IT'S YOUR SHIP

IT'S YOUR SHIP

Management Techniques from the Best Damn Ship in the Navy

CAPTAIN D. MICHAEL ABRASHOFF

FORMER COMMANDER, USS *BENFOLD*

BUSINESS PLUS

NEW YORK   BOSTON

Business Plus
Hachette Book Group
237 Park Avenue
New York, NY 10017
Visit our Web site at www.HachetteBookGroup.com.

Business Plus is an imprint of Grand Central Publishing.
The Business Plus name and logo is a trademark of Hachette Book Group, Inc.

Printed in the United States of America

First Edition: May 2002

28

ISBN 978-0-446-52911-2
Library of Congress Control Number: 2002101310

To the memory of Petty Officer Edward C. Benfold
and to the officers and crew who sailed
in his ship with me.

CONTENTS

CONTENTS

IT'S YOUR SHIP

INTRODUCTION

My story might be called "The Education of USS *Benfold*," which is a guided missile destroyer that I commanded for twenty months beginning in June 1997. Commissioned in 1996 for duty in the Pacific Fleet, the ship is a beautiful fighting machine: 8,600 tons of armor protecting the Navy's most advanced arsenal of computerized missiles; a radar system that can track a bird-size object from fifty miles away; a highly skilled crew of 310 men and women; and four gas turbine engines capable of driving the ship to thirty-plus knots—or more than thirty-three miles an hour—as it speeds into combat, shooting up a huge rooster-tail backwash.

To be given this spectacular vessel as my first sea command was thrilling, but also ironic. Opportunity had called, but in a troubled industry. Our military has spent a lot of time and money preparing for tomorrow's battles with antiquated methods. We continue to invest in the latest technologies and systems, but, as we all know, technology is only a facilitator. The people operating the equipment are what gives us the fighting edge, and we seemed to have lost our way when it came to helping them grow.

The statistics were startling. In years past, nearly 35 percent, or almost 70,000, of the 200,000 people who joined the military annually, wouldn't complete their enlistment contract. Although most left the service involuntarily, doing so was not necessarily a reflection of their character. Of those who completed their first hitch, a very small percentage reenlisted—not nearly enough to keep our senior billets filled. Worse yet, the best talents were often the first to leave. Since it took $35,000 to recruit a trainee and tens of thousands more in additional training costs to get new personnel to the basic level of proficiency, the price of this attrition to the taxpayer was staggering. And that was only the beginning, since the dropouts went home and counter-recruited against us, making it even harder to convince others to join.

We could and should be getting more for our $325 billion a year investment in national defense. In addition to ensuring our safety and security, we should be providing life-forming experiences that shape the characters of young men and women to make them outstanding citizens and contributors to this great country.

Despite her potency, *Benfold* was not as prepared for the threat of attack as she could have been. The dysfunctional ship had a sullen crew that resented being there and could not wait to get out of the Navy. The achievement in my life of which I am the most proud was turning that crew into a tight-knit, smoothly functioning team that boasted—accurately, many felt—that *Benfold* was the best damn ship in the Navy.

I offer my experiences, my successes, and my failures not only because they make a good story, though I think they do. I offer them as a practical guide to any leader in any business or organization. Like the Navy, the business community has to figure out how to help people grow. A recent Gallup study found that when people leave their companies, 65 percent of them are actually leaving their managers. As true in the Navy as it is in business, leaders are failing—and the costs are astounding. Conservative estimates put the cost of losing a trained worker at one and a half times the annual salary of the outgoing employee, as measured by lost productivity and recruiting and training costs for the replacement.

What all leaders have in common is the challenge of getting the most out of our crews, which depends on three variables: the leader's needs, the organization's atmosphere, and the crew's potential competence. In this book, I describe how the Navy and other organizations often mismatch those variables and damage themselves in the process. I am fervently committed to helping any leader at any level, in business or in the military, create the mix that makes those variables 100 percent effective.

Exceptional leaders have always been rare, but they can be made as well as born, and the *Benfold* story is a case in point. But the story also conveys an idea of something far larger than the transformation of one captain and his crew. The terrorist attacks on the United States on September 11, 2001, triggered a global fear of apocalypse from which the rational world can recover only with the aid of inspired leadership at every level of society— churches, families, schools, hospitals, courts, Congress, the White House. Of these, companies and military units are among the organizations most in need of superb leadership, because they drive and guard economic stability. Gravely wounded, but hardly daunted, Americans in business and in the military must now help revive the world economy and win a planetary war without borders.

Crisis spawns leaders, as we saw during those weeks in September when death rained from flawless autumn skies and ordinary people became extraordinary. We may now face a series of crises throughout the world, and the need for steady leaders may be as relentless as the crises themselves.

I hope this book will help anyone suddenly challenged, as I was, with the realization that leadership is earned, not designated.

In a nutshell, hard experience has taught me that real leadership is about understanding yourself first, then using that to create a superb organization. Leaders must free their subordinates to fulfill their talents to the utmost. However, most obstacles that limit people's potential are set in motion by the leader and are rooted in his or her own fears, ego needs, and unproductive habits. When leaders explore deep within their thoughts and feelings in order to understand themselves, a transformation can take shape.

That understanding shifts the leader's perspective on all of the interactions in life, and he or she approaches leadership from a completely different place. As a result, the leader's choices are different from those he or she made when blinded by fear, ego, and habit. More important, others perceive the person as more authentic, which in turn reinforces the new behavior. This can vastly improve how people respond to their leaders and makes their loyalty to the source of gratification more likely: my ship, your company, their peers, the culture that gives their lives meaning and purpose.

To be sure, your organization has a pragmatic goal, and obviously, it isn't to be a therapeutic shelter. My ship's job was war;

your company's purpose is profit. But we will achieve neither by ordering people to perform as we wish. Even if doing so produces short-term benefits, the consequences can prove devastating. My experience has shown that helping people realize their full potential can lead to attaining goals that would be impossible to reach under command-and-control.

While the economy was booming, teeming with high-tech jobs for qualified young people, the Navy was accepting thousands who had thus far been left out of the nation's prosperity. Our job was to turn them into high-tech experts—master operators of state-of-the-art warships costing billions of dollars. Moreover, we had to shape them into self-confident men and women fully able to serve their country in dangerous times and unfamiliar places. We did all this, playing the same hand my predecessor held. We didn't fire or replace anyone. We tapped the potential that had never been recognized.

That *Benfold* succeeded to a startling degree is not necessarily a testament to the U.S. Navy, which is still burdened with a very mixed bag of leaders, but rather to the approach I found, and to my shipmates, who more than justified my trust and confidence in them.

In the chapters that follow, I will detail the ideas and techniques that I used to win my sailors' trust and, eventually, their enthusiastic commitment to our joint goal of making our ship the best in the fleet. The book narrates episodes in *Benfold*'s two-year voyage through uncharted waters of leadership, and is organized around the lessons I learned. A chapter is given to each one: Lead by example; listen aggressively; communicate purpose and meaning; create a climate of trust; look for results, not salutes; take calculated risks; go beyond standard procedure; build up your people's confidence; generate unity; and improve your people's quality of life as much as possible.

At the Naval Academy we studied legendary military leaders, from Alexander the Great to Dwight D. Eisenhower, but I sensed that something was missing from those portraits. Biographers described their victories and heroic gestures, but my years in the Navy taught me that the art of leadership lies in simple things—commonsense actions that ensure high morale and increase the odds of winning.

Leaders must be willing to put the ship's performance ahead of their egos, which for some people is harder than for others. The command-and-control approach is far from the most efficient way to tap people's intelligence and skills. To the contrary, I found that the more control I gave up, the more command I got. In the beginning, people kept asking my permission to do things. Eventually, I told the crew, "It's *your* ship. You're responsible for it. Make a decision and see what happens." Hence the *Benfold* watchword was "It's your ship." Every sailor felt that *Benfold* was his or her responsibility. Show me an organization in which employees take ownership, and I will show you one that beats its competitors.

Captains need to see the ship from the crew's perspective. They need to make it easy and rewarding for crew members to express themselves and their ideas, and they need to figure out how and when to delegate responsibility.

I took command realizing that I could follow either of two courses. One would be to do nothing for two years, lie low, and take no risks. We have all known cold, timid souls; I may have been one myself as I was coming up through the ranks. The problem—the Navy's biggest—is that had I stayed that way and done nothing for two years, I probably still would have been promoted.

The more dangerous course, at least to my career, would be to shake things up, rock the boat to get the truly exceptional performance I felt we needed. And that's what I did. When I came to *Benfold*, I had been on my Navy leadership journey for sixteen years—and what I suddenly realized was that I had the power to do this all along. I just never had the self-confidence.

In business, as in the Navy, there is a general understanding that "they" don't want rules to be questioned or challenged. For employees, the "they" is the managers; for managers, the "they" is the executive cadre. I worked hard at convincing my crew that I did want the rules to be questioned and challenged, and that "they" is "us." One of the ways I demonstrated my commitment was to question and challenge rules to *my* bosses. In the end, both the bosses and my crew listened.

How did I get away with this approach in the notoriously rigid hierarchy of the Navy? One answer is that the Navy was in so much trouble that the brass were desperate enough to give people latitude to try new things. But equally important, I discovered a way to create change without asking a higher authority's permission. In effect, I put myself in the shoes of my boss, then asked, "What do I want from Abrashoff and *Benfold*?" What the boss wanted, I decided, was a ship that met all operational commitments and did so under budget, while achieving high morale and a high retention rate. I thought that if I could deliver these things, my boss would leave me alone. He would concentrate on other ships that weren't delivering the same results.

I also made sure to act in the least threatening manner possible. None of my actions could possibly bankrupt the company or hurt anyone's career. I took prudent, calculated risks, the kind I thought my boss would want me to take. Never once did I do anything to promote myself, just the organization. That way, no one could ever question my motives.

Sure enough, when I got the results I was aiming for, my commodore (the operational commander of a six-ship squadron) was amazed. He started sending other commanding officers over to *Benfold* to figure out what we were doing so they could implement it on their ships. The results improved the business, and my commodore got the credit, so the risks were clearly in his interest. That's the only way to make good things happen in your organization.

Many people consider going out on a limb a sure way to endanger your career, but this conventional wisdom is no way for an organization to stay alive and strong. Organizations should reward risk-takers, even if they fall short once in a while. Let them know that promotions and glory go to innovators and pioneers, not to stand-patters who fear controversy and avoid trying to improve anything. To me, that's the key to keeping an organization young, vital, growing, and successful. Stasis is death to any organization. Evolve or die: It's the law of life. Rules that made sense when they were written may well be obsolete. If so, make them extinct, too.

Of course, trying something new is never easy. For one thing, there aren't any precedents to guide you. But that can be a very good thing.

I gave my first speech at a two-day conference sponsored by the magazine *Fast Company* to six hundred people. I joined Dee Hock, founder of Visa International, and Tom Peters, perhaps best known for his book *In Search of Excellence*. After I talked about *Benfold,* the questions began, and I floundered. The worst one was, "What kind of metrics did you use when you were determining where you wanted to go?"

I stood there like a deer caught in headlights. I was in such a hurry to change the way we did business, I had bypassed conventional business wisdom on how to implement change. The crowd tittered.

Later, I called my sister Connie, who has an MBA and has worked for major financial institutions all over the country. She said the management committee always wants to see the metrics before they allow you to launch new ideas. Since, by definition, new ideas don't have metrics, the result is that great ideas tend to be stillborn in major companies today.

I just knew where *Benfold* was when I arrived, and generally where I wanted us to go from there. If I had been forced to chart a course defined by metrics, the creativity we sparked and the changes we achieved probably could not have happened.

Still, without metrics, how could I decide whether something new was a good idea? There were no guarantees. Life isn't always tidy, and often unintended consequences result from well-meant actions. In general, however, I decided that on just about everything I did, my standard should be simply whether or not it felt right. You can never go wrong if you do "the right thing."

How do you define the right thing? As U.S. Supreme Court justice Potter Stewart said about pornography, you know it when you see it. If it feels right, smells right, tastes right, it's almost surely the right thing—and you will be on the right track.

If that doesn't sound very profound or sophisticated, in the Navy, in business, and in life, it really is as simple as that.

I hope and believe that this book can help leaders of both large and small companies realize that they have the power to be phenomenal leaders, just as I did for many years before I decided to use it. Hopefully, my story will help you develop the confidence. Though a guided missile destroyer isn't Procter & Gamble, the old-line Navy management policies aren't so different from those that still rule most corporations. As a leader, you can change your piece of the world, just as I was able to change mine.

It's your ship.

CHAPTER ONE

TAKE COMMAND

⚓ MY FIRST INKLING OF THE SIZE OF THE JOB CAME AT
1:21 in the afternoon of June 20, 1997, after I formally
assumed command of USS *Benfold*.

When a Navy ship changes hands, all routine work stops two
weeks prior to the event. The crew paints the ship from top to
bottom, sets up a big tent on the flight deck, arranges chairs for
dignitaries, and unrolls a red carpet for the obligatory admiral,
who delivers a speech on the outstanding performance of the
ship's departing skipper. A reception follows. Waves of good feeling saturate the event as the former commanding officer is piped
ashore.

My predecessor was accompanied by his family as he left the
ship. And when the public-address system announced his final

departure, much of the crew was not disappointed to see him go. I can still feel my face flushing with embarrassment when I remember how some didn't give him a respectful send-off.

Truthfully, my first thought as I watched this spectacle was about myself. How could I ensure that my eventual departure wouldn't be met with relief when I left the ship in two years? I was taking over a very tough crew who didn't exactly adore their captain.

The crew would probably dislike me, I thought, if for no other reason than that I represented old-fashioned and perhaps obsolete authority. That was okay; being likable is not high among a ship captain's job requirements. What is essential is to be respected, trusted, and effective. Listening to those raucous jeers, I realized that I had a long way to go before I really took command of *Benfold*.

I knew that I would have to come up with a new leadership model, geared to a new era. And this awkward reception underlined for me just how much the workplace had changed in military as well as in civilian life.

Never before had employees felt so free to tell their bosses what they thought of them. In the long economic boom, people were not afraid of losing their jobs. Other jobs awaited them; even modestly qualified people moved from one company to another in a quest for the perfect position they believed they richly deserved.

However the economy is doing, a challenge for leaders in the twenty-first century is attracting and retaining not just employees, but the best employees—and more important, how to motivate them so that they work with passion, energy, and enthusiasm. But very few people with brains, skills, and initiative appear. The timeless challenge in the real world is to help less-talented people transcend their limitations.

Pondering all this in the context of my post as the new captain of *Benfold,* I read some exit surveys, interviews conducted by the military to find out why people are leaving. I assumed that low pay would be the first reason, but in fact it was fifth. The top reason was not being treated with respect or dignity; second was being prevented from making an impact on the organization; third, not being listened to; and fourth, not being rewarded with more responsibility. Talk about an eye-opener.

Further research disclosed an unexpected parallel with civilian life. According to a recent survey, low pay is also number five on the list of reasons why private employees jump from one company to another. And the top four reasons are virtually the same as in the military. The inescapable conclusion is that, as leaders, we are all doing the same wrong things.

Since a ship's captain can't hand out pay raises, much less stock options, I decided that during my two years commanding *Benfold,* I would concentrate on dealing with the unhappy sailors' top four gripes. My organizing principle was simple: The key to being a successful skipper is to see the ship through the eyes of the crew. Only then can you find out what's really wrong and, in so doing, help the sailors empower themselves to fix it.

A simple principle, yes, but one the Navy applauds in theory and rejects in practice. Officers are told to delegate authority and empower subordinates, but in reality they are expected never to utter the words "I don't know." So they are on constant alert, riding herd on every detail. In short, the system rewards micromanagement by superiors—at the cost of disempowering those below. This is understandable, given the military's ancient insistence on obedience in the face of chaos, which is essential in battle. Moreover, subordinates may sidestep responsibility by reasoning that their managers are paid to take the rap.

A ship commanded by a micromanager and his or her hierarchy of sub-micromanagers is no breeding ground for individual initiative. And I was aiming for 310 initiative-takers—a crew ready, able, and willing to make *Benfold* the top-rated ship in the fleet.

What I wanted, in fact, was a crew that bore at least a dim resemblance to the ship's namesake, Edward C. Benfold, a Navy hospital corpsman who died in action at the age of twenty-one while tending to two wounded Marines in a foxhole during the Korean War. When several enemy soldiers approached the foxhole, throwing grenades into it, Benfold picked up the grenades and stormed the enemy, killing them and himself in the process. He was posthumously awarded the Congressional Medal of Honor. (Incidentally, he came from the small town of Audubon, New Jersey, which has two other Medal of Honor winners as well, making it the highest per capita Medal of Honor city in the United States.) I wanted my crew to display courage and step up to the plate just as Edward Benfold had done.

We had nowhere to go but up. Still, up is not an easy direction. It defies gravity, both cultural and magnetic. So the *Benfold* story is hardly a hymn to our unalloyed success in converting the heathen. It was tough going.

At first, my unconventional approach to the job evoked fear and undermined the authoritarian personality that had been imprinted on the ship. But instead of constantly scrutinizing the members of my crew with the presumption that they would screw up, I assumed that they wanted to do well and be the best.

I wanted everyone to be involved in the common cause of creating the best ship in the Pacific Fleet. And why stop there? Let's shoot for the best damn ship in the whole damn Navy!

I began with the idea that there is always a better way to do things, and that, contrary to tradition, the crew's insights might be more profound than even the captain's. Accordingly, we spent several months analyzing every process on the ship. I asked everyone, "Is there a better way to do what you do?" Time after time, the answer was yes, and many of the answers were revelations to me.

My second assumption was that the secret to lasting change is to implement processes that people will enjoy carrying out. To that end, I focused my leadership efforts on encouraging people not only to find better ways to do their jobs, but also to have fun as they did them. And sometimes—actually, a lot of times—I encouraged them to have fun for fun's sake.

Little gestures go a long way. At our base in San Diego, for example, I decided to quit feeding the crew with official Navy rations, and instead used the ship's food budget to buy quality civilian brands that were cheaper as well as tastier. I sent some of our cooks to culinary school. What they learned turned *Benfold* into a lunchtime mecca for sailors from all over the San Diego base.

There were also our music videos, courtesy of stealth technology. We have all heard of the stealth bomber. We are now building ships using stealth characteristics to minimize our radar signature so that the enemy cannot easily find us. By using angled decks and radar-absorbing materials on the hull, an enemy's radar beam is either deflected or absorbed. As a result, an 8,600-ton, 505-foot-long destroyer looks no bigger on an enemy's radar screen than a fishing boat. The angled superstructure that stealth technology dictated on the after part of Benfold resembles the screen of an old drive-in movie theater. So one of my more resourceful sailors created outdoor entertainment by projecting music videos on that surface, which the refueling crews could enjoy. The shows generated a lot of buzz throughout the fleet and lightened up a tedious and sometimes dangerous job.

While spending thirty-five interminable autumn days in the scorching Persian Gulf, we acquired a lifeboat full of pumpkins, a fruit alien to the Middle East. Our supply officer pulled off this coup, and I thought it would be micromanaging to ask for an explanation. After we overdosed on pumpkin pie, we distributed scores of unused pumpkins for a jack-o'-lantern carving contest.

The innovations weren't all lighthearted. On our way from San Diego to the Persian Gulf, for example, our first stop was Honolulu. *Benfold* accompanied two other ships, USS *Gary* and USS *Harry W. Hill*, both skippered by officers senior to me. The operational commander of all three ships was a commodore aboard *Hill*.

During the seven-day voyage, we performed exercises and drills. On the sixth day, we were supposed to detect and avoid a U.S. submarine that was posing as an enemy. The submarine's task was to find and sink the ship carrying the commodore. Though the commanding officer of *Gary* was in charge of this particular exercise, because of his seniority, three days prior to the exercise no plan had yet been announced, and I sensed an opportunity. In business lingo, you could say *Benfold*'s crew had a chance to boost the ship's market share.

I called my junior sonarmen into my stateroom, along with the appropriate officers to serve as witnesses, and assigned them the task of coming up with an innovative plan. I told them to put themselves in the shoes of the submarine's commanding officer (CO), to figure out what he was going to do, and then to develop a strategy to scupper it.

To everyone's surprise—including mine—they devised the most imaginative plan I had ever seen. We submitted it, but both the commodore and *Gary's* CO shot it down in favor of a last-minute plan based on the same tactics the Navy has been using since World War II. Now more than ever, we must stop preparing for past battles and prepare for new ones.

When I heard their decision, I went ballistic. Forcefully, almost disrespectfully, I argued with them on the ship-to-ship radio. The radio is a secure circuit, but also a party line that any sailor can listen to by punching the right button, which all of my sailors did. They heard me challenge my bosses to try something new and bold. I was told in no uncertain terms that we would use *Gary's* plan. I asked for an NFL instant replay, appealing the decision. Nope. Tradition, plus outmoded business practices, carried the day.

As a result, the submarine sank all three of us—without its crew breaking a sweat. Talk about dejection. But my sailors knew that I had gone to bat for them. I could not do less: They had done the same for me by designing such innovative solutions.

The next day, we were scheduled to pull into Pearl Harbor. Navy ships arrive ashore and depart for sea in order of the date of rank of their commanding officers, another archaic monument to tradition. I was the junior commanding officer on our three ships, so *Benfold* was scheduled to arrive last, at 1700 hours in the late afternoon, and depart first at 0700 the next morning, on our way to Singapore.

Since the submarine exercise (read fiasco) was over early in the morning, I saw no reason to drift at sea waiting for the other ships to precede me into Pearl when my sailors could enjoy a whole day's liberty ashore if we left early. With my crew again listening on the party line, I radioed the other captains and asked if they might want to ask permission to go in early. Nothing doing, they said. Stick to plan. Don't stir up trouble, which is exactly what I did when I called the commodore, over their objections, and asked to go in early. His tone wasn't friendly; he, too, had been listening to my conversations with the other COs.

"Give me a good reason," he said.

"We will save taxpayers' money by not sitting out here wasting fuel. Also, I have a broken piece of equipment I want to have fixed, and finally, I would like my crew to enjoy a day on the beach. By my count, that's three good reasons."

The commodore cleared his throat. Then, to everyone's surprise, he said, "Permission granted."

You could hear my sailors cheering throughout the ship. We revved up all four engines and rooster-tailed to the mouth of the harbor at max speed, hardly saving any fuel! We got our equipment fixed, and by midday my sailors were headed for Waikiki and mai tais. That's when they began saying, "This is not your father's Navy."

And that's when I knew that I had taken command—not just in name, but in truth. One sailor told me that the crew thought I cared more about performance and them than about my next promotion. That's another thing you need to learn about your people: They are more perceptive than you give them credit for, and they always know the score—even when you don't want them to.

A lot of the sailors I worked with came from the bottom rung of the socioeconomic ladder. They grew up in dysfunctional families in blighted neighborhoods, where addiction and abuse were common. They went to lousy schools and had little, if any, of what I took for granted as a kid: stability, support, succor. Still, despite all this adversity and the fact that they had nothing handed to them in life, they were some of the best citizens I have ever met. Unlike them, I didn't have to look very far to find my heroes; I had some in my own family. And the older I get, the more I appreciate, even revere, them.

My paternal grandparents came to the United States from Macedonia in 1906 and settled in Mount Union, Pennsylvania. My father, one of eleven children, served in World War II, as did three of his brothers. In the opening hours of the Battle of the Bulge, my uncle Butch took seven bullets to his helmet, was knocked out, presumed dead, and lay on the ground for three days while the battle raged. When soldiers came through to pick up the bodies, they realized he was still breathing. He recovered, and died just last year at the age of eighty-eight.

My uncle Kero, a paratrooper, jumped behind enemy lines in occupied France on a successful mission to gather intelligence.

My father was in the Army, assigned to the Merchant Marine as a radio operator. At the Brooklyn Navy Yard, he was told to choose between two ships. The first was spanking new and the second was an old rust bucket. Maybe because his sympathies were always with the underdog, my father chose the latter. The Army's record-keeping was poor, and he was listed as being on the new ship, which was sunk by a German U-boat in the North Atlantic on one of its first voyages. The War Department even notified my grandfather that my father was killed in action. The

Army stopped his pay. You can imagine the emotions when my father wrote home and his dad realized that he was still alive. Proving to the Army that he was still alive and requesting that they restart his pay evoked lots of emotions as well.

When I was growing up, my father told us war stories at the noon meal on Sundays. We heard them so many times we could finish each one after hearing the first three words. Still, they had a profound impact on us—probably more than my dad realized.

My mother also contributed to the war effort. Altoona, a railroad hub at that time, handled millions of tons of war supplies. My mother, who later became a teacher, worked a shift at the switching stations keeping the trains running.

My father, uncles, and mother were all powerful role models for me. Like NBC news anchor Tom Brokaw, I consider theirs the greatest generation, and I admire their tremendous sacrifices. I told my crew in my very first speech that I had been running hard every day to fill my father's shoes, and I feel that I still am.

My parents never made much money (my father was a social worker and my mother taught junior high), but that didn't stop them from making my childhood a privileged one. We never knew we were poor. They provided discipline, encouragement, and a lot of love. It added up to stability, symbolized by a marriage that has now lasted for fifty-four years in the same house— the one where my mother was born eighty years ago. I believe any of us fortunate enough to come from stable families have a responsibility to try to understand the experiences of those growing up without support, security, or positive role models.

I was number six of seven children. My parents really struggled to put the first five through college, so when the opportunity came for me to get my education "free" at the U.S. Naval Academy, I jumped at the chance. Being an athlete in high school helped me gain admittance: I was recruited to play football. I turned out to be at best a mediocre football player, so I'm glad I had a day job when I graduated.

My degree was in political science, but 80 percent of the courses at the Naval Academy were in engineering, chemistry, physics, calculus, and other technical subjects, which were excruciating for me. Between that and the sheer competitiveness of the place, I wasn't a stellar student. I was lucky to graduate in the bottom third of the class.

For a Navy officer, your first posting depends on your class rank at the Academy, and if you choose to be a ship driver, as I did, you find that the sleekest, newest ships go to the people at the top of the class. My first assignment was to an old rust bucket of a frigate, USS *Albert David*. Oddly, that turned out to be an advantage. On the fast new ships, the Academy hotshots continued to compete with one another for training time and opportunities to learn. On *Albert David*, competing with officers at the bottom of the list, I still had to bust my butt, but it was easier to break out. I got great opportunities at an early stage in my career that I probably would not have had if I had done better at the Academy.

But the officers I was reporting to were also considered to deserve the *Albert David*, and it was their leadership style I was learning. Unfortunately, that was old-fashioned command-and-control; they barked orders and micromanaged everything. I started as the communications officer, but I got to drive the ship a lot because many of the officers were afraid to try. The captain was abusive. He yelled at us so hard that the veins on his neck and forehead would bulge.

At one point, the captain fired the antisubmarine warfare officer and told me, who had no training at all, to replace him. I was able to do some good things by studying my job and telling my dysfunctional division what to do. I was getting semi-good results and moving up the career ladder, but I was still handicapped by my micromanaging style.

I started to get a broader view in my next post, as an aide to Admiral Hugh Webster in Subic Bay in the Philippines, where I was posted for eighteen months. I sat in on all his meetings and read all his confidential correspondence. I even wrote most of his letters for him, and I learned how a two-star admiral in the U.S. Navy operates. That gave me a top-down view of the organization and how people interact with the upper chain of command. We traveled widely in Asia, planned the first U.S. naval visit to Qingdao, China, since the Chinese revolution, and monitored Soviet naval movements from a ship off Vladivostok. It was a great learning experience.

I was twenty-five years old at the time, and most twenty-five-year-olds don't get the opportunity to see how the organization runs at a senior level. It was good training, which businesses could give their up-and-coming young people by making them executive assistants to the top officers.

My next assignment was to the destroyer USS *Harry W. Hill* as the combat systems officer, which made me a department head and also the tactical action officer in charge of running the combat information center. It was a good ship with a great commanding officer, but the executive officer (XO) was the most command-and-control officer I'd ever experienced in the military. Three weeks after I got to the ship in 1987, he called me into his stateroom when we finished the first exercise and told me flatly that I was the worst tactical action officer he had ever seen in his life. I think his assessment was right, so I took it as notice that I had to get better. It wasn't easy, but when I left the ship eighteen months later, he told me I was the best tactical action officer he had ever seen.

The captain and XO could easily have fired me if they chose to, but I was eager to learn. They saw that I had the right attitude and leadership abilities, and they provided the training I needed in the technical skills. It was rough at the beginning, but they gave me chances, and I benefited. It taught me not to give up on people until I have exhausted every opportunity to train them and help them grow.

From *Harry W. Hill* I went to USS *England*, a guided missile cruiser, where I served from 1989 to 1991. Again, I was combat systems officer, but with a much more complex system; from supervising a crew of 80, I was now managing 120 people. We had a tense tour of duty in the Persian Gulf during Operation Desert Shield, which I will discuss at length later in the book.

When I left *England*, I returned to the Bureau of Naval Personnel to work as an assignment officer. I assigned officers to all the ships in the Atlantic Fleet. It was a staff position, not leadership; I was merely an action officer, doing the work on my own, and I was good at it. The ships were my customers, and I became a master at this process. I was responsible for the Atlantic Fleet, but senior captains from the Pacific Fleet called and told me they had heard that if you wanted anything done at the Bureau, you should call Mike Abrashoff. So I was still climbing the ladder, doing great things; but I was also still relying on my ability to get things done and to micromanage, not on my leadership skills.

I did so well that I was posted as executive officer on the

guided missile cruiser USS *Shiloh,* which was then the most modern ship in the Navy. *Shiloh* was a great ship, and taught me a lot about leadership; it was there that I realized I wanted desperately to become a different kind of leader. But I still didn't know how to accomplish that.

In 1994, I was given the greatest opportunity of my life when I was selected to be the military assistant to Secretary of Defense William Perry. Each of the four services provided three nominees, so I was competing against eleven people for the job. The admiral at the U.S. Bureau of Naval Personnel who submitted my name told me not to get my hopes up. I wasn't the Navy's top pick, he said, and if I got an interview, he hoped I would not embarrass the Navy. Talk about a confidence builder.

Somehow, I got the job—perhaps because my tour with Admiral Webster had taught me how to be a team player and deal confidently with senior officials. However, although I was selected for the job, I was joining a superbly functioning staff, and I was going to have to prove to the team that I was going to be trustworthy—that my first loyalty was to the Office of the Secretary of Defense rather than to my parent service, the U.S. Navy.

There are many highly critical jobs in and around the government that require military officers and some enlisted personnel to be "loaned out" from their parent service (Army, Air Force, Navy, or Marines) to another organization, such as the White House, Joint Chiefs of Staff, or the Office of the Secretary of Defense. The offices that receive the personnel on loan are the policy makers for the national security apparatus, which sometimes has to make policy that is contrary to the parochial interests of each service. In such an instance, pressure by the parent service is applied on these officers on loan to keep the parent service informed of what is being discussed, so that the admirals and generals can mobilize to defeat the change in policy.

It's an insidious practice that causes distrust in the Pentagon. Secretary of Defense Donald Rumsfeld was quoted in *TIME* magazine as saying, "My Lord, in this place, all you have to do is think about something, and it is leaked. It's like there are eavesdropping microphones on your brain."

As a result, newly reporting personnel are not always fully trusted at the beginning. I felt, rightly or wrongly, that initially I had to prove my trustworthiness, not to Dr. Perry, but rather to the rest of the staff. It helped that the late Chief of Naval Operations, Admiral Mike Boorda, took me aside shortly after I got the job and told me that he expected me to be totally loyal to the Secretary of Defense, and if any other admiral put pressure on me to betray a confidence, I could go directly to him, Admiral Boorda, and the problem would be taken care of.

I spent the time watching, listening, and learning how the Pentagon worked. Little by little, people got to know me and began to give me the rotten jobs that no one else wanted but that I was happy to do. In fact, I used to joke that there were three types of missions in the office: the surefire successes (the two-star general kept those), the potential successes, and the surefire failures. Guess which ones I was assigned? The good news is that I was successful at about 75 percent of these hapless assignments. The bad news is that it sometimes took a tire iron to get them done.

One of my main tasks was to keep Secretary Perry on schedule. Like all great leaders, he was truly disciplined. Once he approved the schedule that we proposed, he expected to stick to it, down to the minute. Meetings started on time and ended on time, with resolution; no meeting was spent talking about the need for more meetings.

Senior military officers on the make would often try to extend their face-time with Perry, schmoozing with him to enhance their careers. What they didn't realize was that he saw right through their crude tactics. What they also didn't realize was that someone had to be the gatekeeper and that I, holding the key, could make their lives very miserable.

For example, one time we were in Riyadh, Saudi Arabia, scheduled to meet with the families of five Defense Department employees who had been killed the week before when a car bomb exploded outside their offices. Before seeing them, we were to be briefed on operations by a two-star Air Force general. Although the briefing was important, Perry already had a firm grasp of the issues, and the briefing was less crucial than extending his condolences to the families.

The general's briefing also promoted the general. When he showed no signs of finishing, I cut in, announced the briefing was over, and we were off to meet the families. Secretary Perry left. The general took me by the arm and berated me, but I lit into him in a way that I had never done to a senior officer before. Sometimes desperate measures are needed when you are dealing with a sclerotic bureaucracy.

I learned a lot about institutional politics from that job. I discovered how to save taxpayers' money, made possible by a revision in our acquisition policies. All it took was my willingness to ignore some of the Navy's antiquated guidelines, notably those that wasted tax dollars, which had yet to be updated.

But my brush with the Pentagon bureaucracy focused my attention on something much bigger: the Navy's outgoing tide of good sailors. When I got a ship, I resolved, I would lead it in such a way that that trend would be reversed.

Now, with *Benfold*, it was put up or shut up.

Though I brought with me a lot of negative leadership styles that I learned early in my career, I had already decided that if I was ever going to fill my father's shoes, it was time for me to leave my comfort zone and chart my own course. Luckily, I also had positive role models outside of my family, notably Secretary Perry. It was time to confront everything I had hated about the Navy as I climbed up through its ranks, and fix it all. Though the goal was presumptuous, I told myself that it was important that I try to do this. I might never get promoted again, but I decided that the risk was worth it. I wanted a life I could be proud of. I wanted to have a positive effect on young people's lives. I wanted to create the best organization I could. And I didn't want to squander this leadership opportunity. I have learned over and over that once you squander an opportunity, you can never get it back. When I am ninety years old and hanging out at Leisure World, I don't want to look back on my life and say, "If only I had . . ."

I was terribly insecure, scared, and full of doubt at first. I had never been in such a position before, and I kept asking myself whether or not I was doing the right thing. But I had to make the leap, and I knew I wasn't doing it for myself. I was doing it for my people. I wanted them to have a great experience, and, above all, I never wanted to write parents to say that their son or daughter was not coming home because of something I had done or failed to do. And in the end, I was doing it for the Navy, which I still love even though it had not yet realized that it wasn't "your father's Navy" anymore.

I mean no disrespect when I say that. After all, our fathers' Navy was an extraordinary force that won the biggest sea battles in history. But today's Navy is a different organism. *Benfold,* for instance, is a much more intricate machine than the ships of even twenty years ago. It can deliver far more firepower, with more accuracy, than ten ships combined could in those days. Incredibly complex, the ship emits unprecedented floods of information to be digested, processed, and acted on, sometimes with only seconds to spare. As in business, no one person can stay on top of it all. That's why you need to get more out of your people and challenge them to step up to the plate. What's needed now is a dramatic new way of inspiring people to excel while things are happening at lightning speed.

We achieved that on *Benfold.* I'm not just bragging; the numbers prove it.

In fiscal 1998, we operated on 75 percent of our budget, not because we consciously tried to save money, but because my sailors were free to question conventional wisdom and dream up better ways to do their jobs. For example, we reduced "mission-degrading" equipment failures from seventy-five in 1997 to twenty-four in 1998. As a result, we returned $600,000 of the ship's $2.4 million maintenance budget and $800,000 of its $3 million repair budget. Of course, our reward was to have the Navy's budgeters slash exactly $600,000 and $800,000 from our allotment the following year. Then we saved another 10 percent from that reduced figure, and duly returned it, too.

During this period, *Benfold*'s "readiness indicators" soared. For the hundred days we served in the Persian Gulf during the Iraqi crisis of 1997, we were the go-to ship of the Gulf Fleet, and we got the toughest assignments. We made the highest gunnery score in the Pacific Fleet. We set a new record for the Navy's predeployment training cycle (preparing for our next assignment), which usually requires fifty-two days—twenty-two in port and thirty at sea. We did it in nineteen days—five in port and fourteen at sea—and earned ourselves thirty-three precious days of shore leave.

When I came aboard *Benfold,* the Navy as a whole had a horrible retention rate. Less than half of all sailors reenlisted for a second tour of duty; that they can retire with generous benefits after only twenty years of service tempted few. *Benfold* itself had a truly dismal retention rate—28 percent. In short, the ship was souring nearly three out of four of its youngest sailors, the people the Navy needs most if it is going to develop a critical mass of reliable petty officers and long-term specialists.

How did our approach affect *Benfold's* retention rate? Even I find this startling, but the numbers don't lie. The ship's retention rate for the two most critical categories jumped from 28 percent to 100 percent, and stayed there. All of *Benfold's* career sailors reenlisted for an additional tour. If we had to replace them, we would spend about $100,000 per new recruit for her or his training. And the considerable dollar savings are only the beginning. The ultimate benefit—retaining highly skilled employees—is incalculable.

When I took command of *Benfold,* I realized that no one, including me, is capable of making every decision. I would have to train my people to think and make judgments on their own. Empowering means defining the parameters in which people are allowed to operate, and then setting them free.

But how free was free? What were the limits?

I chose my line in the sand. Whenever the consequences of a

decision had the potential to kill or injure someone, waste tax-payers' money, or damage the ship, I had to be consulted. Short of those contingencies, the crew was authorized to make their own decisions. Even if the decisions were wrong, I would stand by my crew. Hopefully, they would learn from their mistakes. And the more responsibility they were given, the more they learned.

By trading pageantry for performance, we created learning experiences at every turn. We made sure that every sailor had time and was motivated to master his or her job; getting by wasn't good enough.

As a result, we had a promotion rate that was over the top. In the Navy, promotions depend on how well you perform on standardized tests. Everyone ready for advancement takes them at the same time, and those with the highest scores are promoted. When I took command in 1997, my new crew was advancing less than the Navy average. In 1998, I promoted eighty-six sailors, a big leap in self-esteem for roughly one-third of the ship's crew. Now *Benfold* sailors were getting promoted at a rate twice the Navy average.

The fact is that the new environment aboard *Benfold* created a company of collaborators who were flourishing in a spirit of relaxed discipline, creativity, humor, and pride. The Navy noticed: Just seven months after I took the helm, *Benfold* earned the Spokane Trophy, an award established in 1908 by that famous Navy buff President Theodore Roosevelt. It is given each year to the most combat-ready ship in the Pacific Fleet.

Shortly after the award was announced, my boss, the commodore, sent me an e-mail offering congratulations. But don't get too cocky, he warned. His ship had not only won the equivalent award in the Atlantic Fleet, it had also achieved the Navy's all-time highest score in gunnery, 103.6 (out of a possible 105). "Until you can beat my gunnery score," he wrote, "I don't want to hear any crowing from USS *Benfold*."

Two weeks later, we were scheduled to shoot our own gunnery competition. I didn't say a word to my team; I just taped that e-mail to the gun mount. They scored 104.4 of a possible 105 points, after which I let them write a response to the commodore. I didn't read it, but I have the impression that they crowed quite a bit.

Benfold went on to beat nearly every metric in the Pacific Fleet, and frequently the crew broke the existing record. Directly, I had nothing to do with these triumphs. As I saw it, my job was to create the climate that enabled people to unleash their potential. Given the right environment, there are few limits to what people can achieve.

CHAPTER TWO

LEAD BY EXAMPLE

WHILE THE IMAGE OF A NAVY CAPTAIN CONJURES UP gold braid and firmly barked orders, neither of those things makes a leader. A leader will never accomplish what he or she wants by ordering it done. Real leadership must be done by example, not precept.

Whether you like it or not, your people follow your example. They look to you for signals, and you have enormous influence over them. If they see you fail to implement a policy you disagree with, they may think they have a green light to do the same. If they see you not telling the truth, they may feel free to lie as well. Likewise, if they see you challenge outdated business practices, they will follow suit. Doing so will become ingrained in the culture. Whenever an officer proposed a plan, I asked, "Why do we have to do it that way? Is there a better way?" So they always searched for better ways before coming to me. The signals you send are important. You train your crew how to operate through every decision you make and every action you take.

IT'S FUNNY HOW OFTEN THE PROBLEM IS YOU.

Whenever I could not get the results I wanted, I swallowed my temper and turned inward to see if I was part of the problem. I asked myself three questions: Did I clearly articulate the goals? Did I give people enough time and resources to accomplish the task? Did I give them enough training? I discovered that 90 percent of the time, I was at least as much a part of the problem as my people were.

I first learned that lesson in the Philippines, when I was Admiral Webster's aide. Each admiral has his own so-called barge, a nice yacht that can be used for entertaining or just for cruising. Webster had a beautiful barge, and as his aide, I was in charge of it, but I had no staff to maintain it.

One day shortly after we both got to Subic Bay, he decided to take the barge out. I commandeered a couple of sailors from one of the ships in port to staff it, and the admiral and I cruised out to an island off the bay. But on the way back, the boat broke down. We were adrift in the harbor for about an hour. Then our radio died. The admiral said, "Take my flag down." When an admiral is on any kind of boat or ship, it flies his flag, and Admiral Webster didn't want anyone to know he was out there helpless. You can only imagine how humiliated I was. Finally, a garbage barge came by, and I waved it down. The garbage men threw us a rope and towed us back into port as the admiral fumed in the cabin below.

I never saw the admiral as upset as he was that day, and I really felt the heat. I had plenty of excuses—I didn't have the crew or the tools to run the thing properly. But at the end of the day, I was responsible. I should have been more prepared.

Needless to say, for the rest of my term, I put great effort into maintaining the barge, and we never had trouble again.

I have repeatedly learned and relearned that lesson of pre-paredness over the years, and there seems to be no end of ways to fail. My most vivid recollection dates back to 1994, when I was the XO of *Shiloh*. A sailor had fallen asleep while standing watch. This is an extremely egregious offense, because people can get killed if you are not alert. The young sailor was placed on report (think of it as being charged with a crime), and I had to decide whether to send the case to the judge (the commanding officer) or dismiss the charge.

Well, this was an open-and-shut case—if you are asleep on watch, you are guilty. There was no need to bother with the facts. So I sent the sailor to the captain for punishment, without any further investigation.

To my utter surprise, the captain asked the sailor why he had fallen asleep on watch. The sailor said he had been up all night cleaning a dirty workspace. Why did he have to stay up to clean it? Because the chief told him it had to be done by 8 A.M. "Chief, why didn't you give him more time to get it done?" "Because the division officer told me it had to be done." I immediately saw where this was heading and started to sweat. The captain turned to the division officer, who turned to the department head (by this time, I was standing in a puddle), who turned to me and said, "The XO told me to get it done by 8 A.M."

How in the world could I have known that they were so short-handed that they would have to keep somebody up all night to get it finished? But in fact I should have known or at least been approachable enough for the officers to feel safe explaining to me why it was a problematic order. I didn't get all the facts, I didn't realize that there were not enough resources to get the job done in the time I had allowed. The captain dismissed the case and I felt like a complete, uncaring idiot. Never again, I promised myself, would I give an order without clearly articulating the goal, providing the time and resources to get it done, and ensuring that my crew had the proper training to do it right.

But, of course, there would be a next time. You never know all the things you should know.

NEVER FORGET YOUR EFFECT ON PEOPLE.

Leaders need to understand how profoundly they affect people, how their optimism and pessimism are equally infectious, how directly they set the tone and spirit of everyone around them.

How many times have you gone into your boss's office and felt smaller? For example, she is working on e-mail and doesn't even acknowledge your presence; or the boss is talking to you and keeps interrupting to pick up the phone, because the phone is more important than talking to you. Or worse yet, he belittles you or your efforts.

Mediocre leaders don't even take the trouble to know their people. I learned of an incident between my predecessor on *Ben-*

fold and then-Seaman Blaine Alexander of Texas. It was near the end of the captain's tour when he stopped Blaine in the passageway and asked if he was new to the ship. Now Blaine was one of the first to report to *Benfold* as she was being built and had served two years under that captain. But he answered, with a straight face, "Why, yes sir, I am. And what is it that you do aboard the ship?" My predecessor then fingered his gold command-at-sea pin and said, "Do you see this pin? This means I'm the commanding officer of this ship." Blaine responded that it was a pleasure to meet him. A couple of sailors who witnessed this exchange almost split their guts laughing.

As a manager, the one signal you need to steadily send to your people is how important they are to you. In fact, nothing is more important to you. Realize your influence, and use it wisely. Be there for your people. Find out who they are. Recognize the effects you have on them and how you can make them grow taller.

When I left *Benfold,* I became an aide to a senior civilian executive. Whenever my boss could not attend the Monday board of directors' meeting, I was tagged to take his place. These meetings were difficult because the man who ran them didn't handle criticism particularly well, especially if it involved his immediate staff. If you pointed out deficiencies in his operation, his defenses kicked in and he wound up arguing with everyone in the room. I don't think he understood the silencing effect he had on people—it was as though he was sending a message: My operation is perfect; no need for improvement.

Although he is hugely talented, it seemed to me that his response to criticism wasn't helping us address deep-seated problems in the organization. I tried to think of some way to help. I decided to send him a private e-mail, in which I tried to tactfully describe how his outbursts stifled progress and cast a pall over the discussions. I suggested that he consider trying to reflect on his responses.

Guess what: I got an e-mail back from him saying something to the effect of, "You're right. I didn't realize the effect I was having on people. Now that you have pointed it out, I will be a lot more restrained." And he actually started to improve. If I had confronted him in public, the results would have been devastating.

I had nothing to gain and everything to lose by sending the e-mail, which in itself is a key to my success in challenging senior people. I made it clear that my only agenda was helping the Navy improve, with all due credit to my superiors, not to myself. If I were viewed as a self-promoter, I would have been squashed long before I had a chance to command a ship. It helps when your motives are pure and you make sure they come across that way.

It is well-known that every leader sets the tone for his or her organization. Show me an enthusiastic leader, and I will show you an enthusiastic workforce. And vice versa: If the leader has a bad day, the whole organization has a bad day.

But what do you do on the days when you just can't be cheerful and positive? The key is to minimize the damage you impose. My crew called it the "dark side." A ship at sea is a 24/7 operation, and I am always on call if problems arise. The officers noticed that the more I was called during the night and the less sleep I got, the crankier I was the next day. They kept track of how often I was called, and if it was four or more times in one night, or if I had to get out of my bunk to supervise something, they knew the next day would not be pleasant. I later found out that after reveille (6 A.M.), word would spread about how often I had been awakened. After one sleepless night, a nineteen-year-old sailor came up to me as I was sitting on the bridge wing chair and said, "Cap'n, word has it that the dark side is going to be out today." I still chuckle over that incident. The lesson to be learned, though, is that everybody has a dark side, and the more you understand it, the better you can manage it. I decided to minimize interaction with my crew on days when the dark side was evident, so that at least I would do no harm.

LEADERS KNOW HOW TO BE HELD ACCOUNTABLE.

Throughout my years in the Navy, there were several times in which accidents happened or mistakes were made—tricky, onboard maneuvers; moving heavy equipment; tactical exercises; and the like. Quite honestly, many of these mishaps were difficult to avoid due to the massive amount of equipment involved. That being said, they cost as much as millions of dollars in taxpayers' money to rectify and make repairs.

When these accidents did occur, I was struck by how often everyone tried to put the best spin on it or somehow tried to shield themselves from being held accountable. That's probably just human nature—no one wants to be blamed for a major screwup. But I've always believed that leaders know when to stand up and be held accountable.

Personally, I'd like to live in a culture that allows people to candidly acknowledge mistakes and take responsibility. It's far more useful to focus on making sure the accident never happens again, rather than on finding someone to blame. As a captain, I didn't want to foster a culture that shows the lower ranks that the upper ranks try to gloss over problems to avoid blame or save their careers.

NEVER FAIL THE <u>WASHINGTON POST</u> TEST.

When I took over *Benfold,* there was no doubt I wanted it to be the best ship in the history of the Navy. But it was also important for me to get there the right way. I was always careful never to take any ethical shortcuts. My self-test was simple, and it allowed me to decide whether to go or stop in terms of obvious consequences. I just asked myself this: If what I'm about to do appeared on the front page of the *Washington Post* tomorrow, would I be proud or embarrassed? If I knew I would be embarrassed, I would not do it. If I'd be proud, I knew I was generally on the right track.

Getting somewhere is important. How you get there is equally important. And however unsophisticated it seems, as I have said before, the Sunday school standard is enough: Do the right thing. Forget petty politics, don't worry about whether you're going to upset anyone or ruffle anyone's feathers; if it is the right thing to do, figure out a way to get past the egos, a way to get around the bureaucratic infighting, and then do it.

Often, even in hindsight, you can't be 100 percent sure that you did the right thing. When in doubt, go with your gut. I did that for one of my officers on *Benfold,* and I'm glad of it.

Because everyone is needed in combat, nobody gets annual leave while a ship is at sea. The one exception is for sailors with critically ill family members. We fly people home for that. We usually don't let people go home for the birth of a child, but one of my most important officers asked me to make an exception. His wife was due to deliver three days after we left San Diego for the Persian Gulf, which meant that if he left the ship, he would miss the critical exercise we were planning to perform on the way to Honolulu.

I agonized over this for a long time. Many men had missed the births of their children, and I didn't want to give an officer a break that I could not give to the crew. Finally, I decided I would take the risk. From the Navy's point of view, it probably wasn't a good decision, and in fact I think my second in command had talked me into it.

Four days after we left, the baby was born in critical condition, and whether he would live remained unclear for an entire month. In Navy terms, it was now a justifiable leave since the baby was in critical condition. The officer didn't miss just a week of sea duty, but a full six weeks. As I look back, I am eternally thankful that he was there to help his wife and newborn son. We did the right thing by that officer. And the young boy, who is now four years old, is flourishing.

And if the whole story had been printed in the *Washington Post,* I would not have been one bit ashamed.

I also changed the policy on leaves for births. From now on, both officers and enlisted personnel would be flown home for the birth of a child unless we were actually in combat.

OBEY EVEN WHEN YOU DISAGREE.

Every so often your chain of command comes up with a policy that you disagree with—yet it's your responsibility to enforce it. It's important to make your objections known in a private manner with your bosses. But if you lose your argument, it's also important that you carry out that order as if you supported it 100 percent.

This discipline is crucial in battle, of course. A captain's orders can't be ignored; they're vital for saving lives or ships. If I have a missile coming at me and I give the order to fire, I need to have the utmost confidence that my crew will carry it out without delay.

It's important that you not undermine your superiors. In any organization, your people need to know that you support your chain of command. If they see you freelancing, they will feel free not to support you when they disagree with your policies.

After hearing my sea stories and leadership notions, some people assume that I spent my Navy career flouting authority and toying with slow-witted admirals. Nothing could be further from the truth. I was neither a maverick nor a managerial guerrilla. I operated entirely within the parameters laid out for naval officers. I had command of my own ship, but at the end of the day I was nothing more than a mid-level manager in a 400,000-person organization.

That I had strong feelings about the Navy's personnel policies and hoped I could contribute to their being changed doesn't mean that I harbored fantasies that I could change them all by myself. No, the best course was to make the most of what I was given—a chain of command that led upward toward the people actually empowered to enact my ideas once they accepted them.

When I was given a task I did not agree with, I would sometimes ask my people if they thought there was a better way to accomplish the goals that my boss had set. There is nothing wrong with trying to offer a better way to meet a requirement that has been imposed on you. My superiors appreciated my honesty. If I could come up with an improvement, they usually listened to me. In the end, they got credit for the accomplishment—which suited me just fine. It gave them the best possible reason for doing what I wanted to do.

CHAPTER THREE

LISTEN
AGGRESSIVELY

⚓ My education in leadership really began when I was in Washington, watching William Perry in action. He was universally loved and admired by heads of state, by ministers of defense and foreign affairs, and by our own and our allies' troops. A lot of that was because of the way he listened. Each person who talked to him had his complete, undivided attention. Everyone blossomed in his presence, because he was so respectful, and I realized I wanted to affect people the same way.

Perry became my role model, but that wasn't enough to change my leadership style. Something bigger had to happen, and it did. It was painful, but crucial for my realization, that listening doesn't always come naturally to me. Perry opened my eyes to how I often just pretended to hear people. How many times, I asked myself, had I barely glanced up from my work when a subordinate came into my office? I wasn't paying attention; I was marking time until it was my turn to give orders.

That revelation led me to a new personal goal. Shortly after I took command of *Benfold*, I vowed to treat every encounter with every person on the ship as the most important thing at that moment. It wasn't easy for me, and I didn't do it perfectly, but my crew's enthusiasm and smart ideas kept me going.

SEE THE SHIP THROUGH THE CREW'S EYES.

It didn't take me long to realize that my young crew was smart, talented, and full of good ideas that frequently came to nothing because no one in charge had ever listened to them. Like most organizations, the Navy seemed to put managers in a transmitting mode, which minimized their receptivity. They were conditioned to promulgate orders from above, not to welcome suggestions from below.

I decided that my job was to listen aggressively and to pick up every good idea the crew had for improving the ship's operation. Some traditionalists might consider this heresy, but it's actually just common sense. After all, the people who do the nuts-and-bolts work on a ship constantly see things that officers don't. It seemed to me only prudent for the captain to work hard at seeing the ship through the crew's eyes. My first step was trying to learn the names of everyone aboard. It wasn't easy. Try attaching 310 names to 310 faces in one month.

At two o'clock one morning, I woke up suddenly and said to myself, "The only way I can create the right climate is to tell every sailor, in person, that this is the climate I want to create." I decided to interview each crew member on the ship so he or she could hear my expectations directly.

I raced to work that morning, and, without informing my chain of command, I began to interview five crew members a day, one at a time.

I didn't know where I was headed when I started the interviews. I just knew I was desperate to set a different tone. I started with very basic questions: their names; where they were from; their marital status. Did they have children? If so, what were their names? (In time, I came to know not only my crew's names, but those of their spouses as well). Then I asked about *Benfold*: What did they like most? Least? What would they change if they could?

I tried to establish a personal relationship with each crew member. I wanted to link our goals, so that they would see my priority of improving *Benfold* as an opportunity for them to apply their talents and give their jobs a real purpose.

My interviews included more detailed questions: Did they have special memories from high school? How about from their hometowns? I asked if they had goals for their time in the Navy; what about for the future? I always asked them why they had joined the Navy. Until this point, I never knew why people signed up. I learned by listening that 50 percent enlisted because their families could not afford to send them to college, and 30 percent joined to get away from bad situations at home—drugs, gangs, and other violence, for example. Some of their stories broke my heart.

One sailor was raised by a distant relative after his parents were killed in a car accident when he was very young. Another grew up in a neighborhood where gunfire at night was not an uncommon occurrence. Yet another sailor's family were immigrants who arrived in this country with nothing and worked any jobs they could get to support their children.

In just about every case, my sailors were not born with anything remotely resembling a silver spoon in their mouths. But each and every one of them was trying to make something meaningful of their lives. This is one of the greatest strengths of our all-volunteer military force. They are all good, young, hardworking men and women. They deserve nothing but our respect and admiration.

Something happened in me as a result of those interviews. I came to respect my crew enormously. No longer were they nameless bodies at which I barked orders. I realized that they were just like me: They had hopes, dreams, loved ones, and they wanted to believe that what they were doing was important. And they wanted to be treated with respect.

I became their biggest cheerleader. How can you treat people poorly when you know and respect them? How can you put people down when you realize that the journey they are on will not only improve the workplace and help you, but will improve society as well? I enjoyed helping them figure out what they wanted in life and charting a course to get there.

Most of these sailors had never been in a commanding officer's cabin before. But once they saw that the invitation was sincere, the response was overwhelming. I had a microphone for the ship's public-address system on my desk. Whenever I got a good suggestion, I hit the button and told the whole ship about it. I didn't have to go through a management committee—the turnaround time for launching a good idea was about five minutes.

From those conversations, I compiled two lists of all the jobs performed on the ship. List A consisted of all our mission-critical tasks. On list B were all our non-value-added chores—the dreary, repetitive stuff, such as chipping and painting.

I tackled list B with gusto. One sailor I interviewed early on reminded me that we repainted the ship six times a year. Every other month, my youngest sailors—the ones I most wanted to connect with—had to spend entire days sanding down rust and repainting the ship. It was a huge waste of time and effort, mental as well as physical, and a drain on morale to boot.

The sailor suggested a better way: Use stainless steel bolts and nuts to replace the ferrous-metal ones that streaked rust down the sides of the ship. Great idea, I said. Then we checked the Navy supply system. Sorry, no stainless steel fasteners in stock. Pushing the envelope, we went shopping at the nearest Home Depot (as well as a few other stores), and used the ship's credit card to pick up thousands of dollars' worth of stainless steel fasteners. Once installed, they got us out of painting for nearly a year. By the way, the entire Navy has now adopted stainless steel fasteners for installation on every ship.

Next we investigated every piece of removable metal that was topside on the ship and was susceptible to corrosion. There was a relatively new process for preserving the metal that involved baking it to remove surface impurities, then flame-spraying it with a rust-inhibiting paint. This highly effective process was already in use by the Navy, but the facilities to do it were so small that it was impossible to treat even a fraction of what was required. So we found a steel-finishing company in San Diego that could do the job. The entire process cost $25,000, and the paint job was guaranteed to last for years. The sailors never touched a paintbrush again. With more time to learn their jobs, they began boosting readiness indicators all over the ship. The Navy has since dramatically increased the capacity to do this for every ship.

FIND ROUND PEOPLE FOR ROUND HOLES.

The interviews gave me the data that enabled me to match my crew members' personal and professional goals with the tasks that needed to be done. Sometimes you have tasks that don't fit traditional job descriptions. When I searched the database in my head, I realized I had someone whose interests dovetailed with a particular assignment.

Knowing my people well was a huge asset, a lever that helped them do well, even when performing onerous jobs.

I began learning that lesson while I was the executive officer aboard USS *Shiloh*. The job is one of the most dreaded in the Navy because, in addition to being second in command, the XO is also in charge of the entire bureaucracy and paperwork for the ship. *Shiloh* had a crew of 440 people, which means evaluations, performance records, training records, pay records, medical records, dental records, and records about records for 440 people. I shudder to think how many trees die per year just to support the paper requirements for one ship. My main admin assistant was a fellow who got promoted only because he had been around longer than anyone else. He could not type, could not proofread, and could not use a spellchecker—and the few things he could do, he did very slowly. One day he went on vacation, leaving me adrift in a sea of paper that had more errors than you could imagine.

But then a junior seaman, David Lauer, twenty-one, arrived on board. He had been transferred from the ship's administrative office because he could not fit in. Worse, this young man had recently been charged with insubordination. So I expected little or nothing, hoping against hope that he could somehow reduce the administrative mess and free me up for the real mission of a guided missile cruiser—combat readiness.

I met him and briefly explained his duties to him. Soon after, I saw that piles of fitness reports and training records were moving from the disheveled corner of my stateroom to the "For Signature" box on my desk. Miraculously, the stacks of paper were disappearing. Words were spelled correctly; sentences actually had subjects and verbs the *first time;* and I found myself handling paperwork only once. I was dumbstruck.

One day I asked David why he had been kicked out of the administrative office. "I feel as though the chief petty officer hates me," he replied. He explained that within a month of reporting to the ship, he was suggesting ways of improving the efficiency and processes of the office, and the chief didn't like it. After hitting brick walls over and over again because of his junior rank, David had just given up and decided that it was no use.

Well, this was just the kind of independent thinker I needed, and I made him my principal assistant, bypassing five more-senior people. Eventually, David would come to me with an officer's fitness report and say, "XO, wouldn't this sound better if you changed this paragraph to this?" And usually, he'd already have it changed for me to sign right there. Give me performance over seniority any day of the week.

USE THE POWER OF WORD MAGIC.

It would be difficult for me to overstate William Perry's influence on me. He helped me grow dramatically, both as a leader and as a person. The second important lesson he taught me was about the power of language to affect morale. If leaders back their words with action, if they practice what they preach, their words create a self-fulfilling prophecy. Call it "word magic."

In 1996, when China was amassing missiles to shoot at Taiwan, we sent two aircraft carrier battle groups to the region. Secretary Perry happened to be testifying on Capitol Hill and a senator asked him about the buildup. As part of his response, he said he wasn't worried because we had "the best damn Navy in the world." It was reportedly a huge vote of confidence and a morale boost for the Navy, which had been lurching from one mishap to the next. The words became Perry's catchphrase.

I decided *Benfold* was going to be the best damn ship in that Navy. I repeated it to my sailors all the time, and eventually they believed it themselves. I told them I wanted them to greet every visitor who came on board by looking him or her in the eye, shaking hands, smiling, and saying, "Welcome to the best damn ship in the Navy." Visitors loved it. They would make a special effort to search me out and tell me what a wonderful experience it was to deal with my crew. For me, that's how you increase market share and make your business grow. If we were alongside another ship, we'd turn on the PA system and broadcast a greeting from the best damn ship in the Navy. To be truthful, no ship is ever designated "the best in the Navy," so some of the other ships resented the boast, but I wanted my people to believe in themselves.

Sure, it was corny. But it worked, because confidence is infectious. If we weren't actually the best just yet, we were certainly on our way there.

We had another saying on the ship: "The sun always shines on *Benfold*." People began to believe that, too.

CHAPTER FOUR

COMMUNICATE PURPOSE AND MEANING

THE WHOLE SECRET OF LEADING A SHIP OR MANAGING a company is to articulate a common goal that inspires a diverse group of people to work hard together. That's what my sailors got: a purpose that transformed their lives and made *Benfold* a composite of an elite school, a lively church, a winning football team, and—best of all—the hottest go-to ship in the U.S. Navy.

When I took command, I kept walking around the ship trying to understand why everything seemed so desperately wrong, why there was no energy anywhere. It finally hit me that people were just showing up to collect a paycheck every two weeks. They were locking their passion and enthusiasm inside their cars in the parking lot and just bringing their bodies to work. I wanted them to be energized when they came aboard. I wanted them to have as much fun from nine to five every day at work as they did from five to nine every night at home.

I realized what was missing: No one had ever thought to give them a compelling vision of their work, a good reason to believe it was important. After all, we dedicate 60 to 70 percent of our waking hours to this thing called work. It would be terrible if we didn't believe that what we were doing made a difference.

So we spent some time and thought, and came up with a compelling vision that they could believe in. We began making improvements. And slowly they stopped leaving their enthusiasm in their cars and began bringing it to work.

MAKE YOUR CREW THINK "WE CAN DO ANYTHING."

On *Benfold* we used every possible means of communication, including private e-mail to key superiors; daily newsletters for the crew; my own cheerleading for good ideas and walking around the ship chatting; and topside light shows and loud music that expressed *Benfold*'s exuberance. We also issued a steady stream of readiness missives for tasks that ranged from air defense to sea blockades. When we were leaving the Persian Gulf after our hundred-day tour of duty, Vice Admiral Tom Fargo (commander of the Persian Gulf's Fifth Fleet) took me aside and said that I was the only commanding officer who ever wrote ten-page messages on how to improve our procedures. He also said that these messages were the only ones he ever got that were worth reading from beginning to end. Our whole ship became a medium, sending a message of achievement and can-do optimism to the entire fleet.

Unlike my former commander, who chewed people out publicly, I often used *Benfold's* PA system to praise people, share new ideas, explain our goals, and keep everyone working together for a common cause. I used the PA system so much that I later found out that the crew called me "Mega Mike." They said I never met a microphone I could resist talking into.

Like any other workforce, mine appreciated hearing from top management. That communication is another thing missing from many organizations today—managerial silence seems to be growing just when fierce competition is forcing companies to reinvent themselves constantly. Change frightens workers, and their fears thrive in silence. The antidote is obvious: Keep talking. Tell everyone personally what's in store for him or her—new goals, new work descriptions, new organizational structure, and yes, job losses, if that's the case. Explain why the company is making the changes. People can absorb anything if they are not deceived or treated arrogantly. Lies and arrogance create an us-versus-them atmosphere that poisons productivity.

I decided that before I launched any big new policy, I would ask myself how my sailors saw it. If it made sense from that vantage, I probably had a pretty good policy. If it made no sense, I either had the wrong policy or I wasn't communicating clearly. If I had communicated clearly, people would understand, before they got involved, why a new policy was in everyone's best interest, which was how we got the crew's 100 percent support for nearly every change we made.

Some leaders feel that by keeping people in the dark, they maintain a measure of control. But that is a leader's folly and an organization's failure. Secrecy spawns isolation, not success. Knowledge is power, yes, but what leaders need is collective power, and that requires collective knowledge. I found that the more people knew what the goals were, the better buy-in I got—and the better results we achieved together.

OPEN UP THE CLOGGED CHANNELS.

As I rose through the ranks in the Navy, I was continually frustrated by how information was stopped at mid-level regions. I knew that messages being passed down the chain of command would often be stopped on the way, so that people on the bottom didn't get the word. They continued doing what they thought was required, only to be chewed out. Nothing could be more irritating.

I decided that when I took command, I would focus on creating communication that actually conveyed information. My reasoning was selfish and simple: There was a direct relationship between how much the crew knew about a plan and how well they carried it out. That, in turn, brought better results and helped us become more combat-ready.

Sometimes the communications problems were serious, and one equipment snafu nearly scuppered the whole Gulf fleet in the Iraqi crisis of 1997. Of all the communications triumphs during my *Benfold* years, I'm proudest of the work of Radioman First

Class John Rafalko from Wilkes-Barre, Pennsylvania. By thinking out of the box, Rafalko singlehandedly unclogged that monstrous blockage.

By 1997, the way Navy ships communicated at sea had fallen far behind the digital revolution. Although the military services were the first to use satellites for communication, we never foresaw the quantum increase in the need for information. One of the main deficiencies in the 1991 Desert Storm operation against Saddam Hussein was our inability to get huge amounts of information to those on the front lines. We had never invested in increasing the pipeline capacity. The system was certainly secure: You could send top-secret information, because, unlike Internet transmissions, the material was highly encrypted. Unfortunately, the pipelines clogged up with urgent messages that never got delivered.

During the Iraqi crisis of 1997, this backlog developed to the point that, at any given time, as many as 7,000 operational messages might go astray or just stop moving. Some didn't reach their destinations for as many as five or six days, leaving captains out of the loop. Some messages were lost altogether. People on our leading air defense ship were so frustrated with the logjam that they began using a commercial satellite system to transmit encrypted data—at a cost of $10.50 a minute.

The irony was that *Benfold* and many other ships had been equipped with a new satellite system designed for voice communication and the rapid data transmission needed for launching Tomahawks. Unfortunately, how this system worked was somewhat of a mystery to most radio operators, none of whom had been trained to use it properly, much less capitalize on its capabilities. Enter *Benfold*'s radioman John Rafalko.

John spent hours reading all the technical manuals on the new system. Then he told me it could solve all our communications problems for the entire Persian Gulf. This was definitely news that I felt the three-star admiral needed yesterday. But, adhering to my principle of working within the system, we first reported Rafalko's idea to the two-star admiral's chief of staff for communications, who didn't think it would work. The chief of staff indicated he was concerned that implementing the idea would divert needed manpower, and he didn't feel comfortable using the system for a different purpose from that for which it was designed.

Six weeks later, with the leviathans of the U.S. fleet on the verge of becoming incommunicado, I went ahead and sent the two-star admiral (my battle group commander) an urgent message detailing the need for Rafalko's idea and explaining why I thought it would work. He bought into it, ordering the idea put into action immediately.

In no time, we were flying John Rafalko all over the Gulf to train other ships to use the system. He became our jet-setting superstar, whom we were extremely proud of. Our first-class petty officer calmly updated all the gold-braided communications experts.

The new system kicked right in and worked perfectly. The backlog problem disappeared virtually overnight. The system's pipes were so big and transmission was so clear that you could send oceans of messages. Ships suddenly communicated with one another around the clock, without a glitch.

My only role in this saga was to listen to Rafalko, appreciate his idea, and do my best to press it once I was convinced it was a good one. The force of his talent and thinking did everything else. My only regret was that I was not more forceful sooner in pushing his idea through. This is an example of a time when I should have bypassed the bureaucracy and not tolerated a six-week delay.

What this one radioman did for the Navy was phenomenal. He pulled us out of a crisis in wartime and exponentially increased our effectiveness throughout the Persian Gulf and the world. When we returned to San Diego, we were asked to debrief the commander of the Third Fleet, a three-star admiral. This top-level meeting consisted only of senior officers—and John Rafalko. Since it was his idea, I took him along to explain it. I was never more proud of anyone than when young Rafalko became the teacher and the three-star became the pupil. The admiral was clearly impressed with John's description of his new procedure. In *Benfold*'s Navy, talent knows no rank.

When he left *Benfold*, John Rafalko wasn't allowed to fade back into obscurity. The White House quickly grabbed him to help ensure state-of-the-art communications for the president of the United States.

John's story proves that no matter how fantastic your message is, if no one is receiving it, you aren't communicating. You must have mastery of all means of communication, along with the willingness to use them—otherwise, you're just talking to yourself.

AFTER CREATING A GREAT BRAND, DEFEND IT.

While we were in the Persian Gulf, my crew of 310 built a collective reputation that made *Benfold* the star ship of the Fifth

Fleet. Everything we did—from empowering sailors to sharp-shooting Tomahawk missiles—seemed to become a fleet news event that dominated our admiral's morning briefing. Modesty fails to prevent me from savoring those heady times. On the diplomatic front, whenever a mission required finesse and expertise, the fleet commanders sent *Benfold*. Operationally, when they wanted a flawless job performed posthaste, they dispatched *Benfold*. On the morale front, when they wanted to boost the fleet's spirits, they tried to emulate our irreverence, our belly laughs, our zany entertainments—in short, our offbeat prescription for turning hot, bored, sullen sailors into happy warriors.

We wanted to protect our terrific reputation and make sure we gave no ammunition to our potential detractors. My rules for shore-leave behavior in foreign ports were strict, clear, consistent, and non-negotiable. Anyone who discredited USS *Benfold* would be restricted to the ship for the remainder of the deployment. As I saw it, every person in the U.S. military represents the United States. We were all ambassadors, and we had to behave accordingly. I simply would not jeopardize our reputation, so I had zero tolerance for misbehavior. I didn't threaten or make speeches on the subject. I just made the consequences very clear.

In Bahrain, for example, my sailors hung out at the base bar and kept a close eye on the social temperature. The base security people said they could always tell *Benfold* sailors because they were the best behaved. One night, a serious fight, resulting in casualties, broke out between juiced-up sailors from two other ships. The three-star's briefing reported that *Benfold* sailors refused to have anything to do with the rumble. As usual, they were clustered in a group on the far side of the bar, not getting involved.

Maybe my crew's off-duty demeanor wasn't entirely voluntary. But we all liked the result. Whenever trouble broke out ashore, you could always rest assured that *Benfold* sailors would run from it, preserving the ship's well-earned reputation as a trustworthy ambassador.

FREEDOM CREATES DISCIPLINE.

My interviews with the crew worked to empower my sailors to think and act on their own. But equally important, if not more so, was our follow-up process. In the interest of full disclosure and giving credit where credit is due, I will admit that I lifted this idea from the Army. Yes, the Army: Even a broken clock is right twice a day, and this idea was a keeper. It's called the After Action Review, or AAR. After every major decision, event, or maneuver, those involved gathered around my chair on the bridge wing and critiqued it. Even if things had gone well, we still analyzed them. Sometimes things go right by accident, and you are left with the dangerous illusion that it was your doing. We documented what we were trying to do, how we did it, what the conditions and variables were, and how we could improve the process in the future.

The ground rules for these sessions were that you checked your ego at the door, and that there was no retribution for any comments. I encouraged people to challenge or criticize anyone in the group; the most junior seaman could criticize the commanding officer. And they certainly took me up on that. One seaman told me, "Captain, your ship handling stunk today, and it made us do extra work."

Horrors, you may say. Whatever happened to taut captains and tight ships? Bring back the cat-o'-nine-tails. But intrepid sailors win wars; intimidated sailors lose them. Like most businesses, in the Navy there is no fat left on the bone. We no longer enjoy having extra people hanging around to take up slack. We have to get the mission accomplished with limited resources. The only way to do this is with a ruthlessly efficient organization. And if I was causing unnecessary work, then I wanted to know about it. If the crew had a problem with what I was doing, I wanted them to tell me so I could fix it or explain why I had to do things that way, thus expanding my crew's knowledge of limitations or requirements imposed on me.

When people saw me opening myself to criticism, they opened themselves up. That's how we made dramatic improvements. People could get inside one another's minds. They could work together for the best possible *Benfold*. The result? We never made the same mistake twice, and everyone involved got to understand the big picture.

To be honest, when I started my new leadership model, I was pretty anxious about its effect on military discipline. After all, when you let people out of prison, you have no idea how they will respond to their newfound freedom. I kept looking for clues: Was I really just creating anarchy? But quite the opposite happened. To my continued amazement, discipline actually improved under my regime.

During my last twelve months in command, I had many fewer disciplinary cases than my predecessor. With one exception, I never fired or reassigned anyone. The exception was a sailor who had been caught smoking marijuana before I arrived. When the results of his urinalysis arrived, I had no choice but to throw him out; the sentence was mandatory at the time.

There was a corresponding dramatic drop in workmen's compensation cases, which can be an easy way for disgruntled sailors to be reassigned to a hospital; safety-related mishaps almost disappeared (we went from thirty-one to only two). When people feel they own an organization, they perform with greater care and devotion. They want to do things right the first time, and they don't have accidents by taking shortcuts for the sake of expedience.

Previously, people were fighting to get off the ship. Now they were fighting to stay aboard. That kind of desire translates into performance. I am absolutely convinced that with good leadership, freedom does not weaken discipline—it strengthens it. Free people have a powerful incentive not to screw up.

CHAPTER FIVE

CREATE A CLIMATE
OF TRUST

⚓ ONCE LEADERS HAVE SET THE TERMS OF THE NEW SO-
cial contract with their workers, they need to have the
courage of their convictions. The best way to keep a ship—or any
organization—on course for success is to give the troops all the
responsibility they can handle and then stand back. Trust is a
human marvel—it not only sustains the social contract, it's the
growth hormone that turns green sailors into seasoned shipmates
and troubled companies into dynamic competitors.

But trust is a kind of jujitsu: You have to earn it, and you earn
trust only by giving it. Here are the hard lessons I learned.

NEVER PIT DOG AGAINST DOG.

When I took over *Benfold,* I found distrust throughout the ship. The competition to be named commander of a ship is fierce in the Navy, and the four department heads on *Benfold* were competing to get the highest rankings. In most ships, only the top two will ever get their own command. This adversarial relationship is built into the system, and it poisons the whole atmosphere. It divides the crew into factions, erodes their trust in one another, and reduces combat readiness. Growing up, I could never figure out why my commanding officers would tolerate this. For the life of me, I don't see why senior managers in business do so either. Internal bickering and posturing does nothing for the bottom line.

One of the first things I did was to tell the four heads that their futures in the Navy depended on the overall success of *Benfold.* I said they had to believe that they would get bonus points from the selection boards if they worked together to turn *Benfold* into the best damn ship in the Navy. Together we would sink or swim. It does no good to have the best weapons department in the Navy if the engineering department can't make the propellers turn and get us to the fight. All four have been screened for executive officer duties and are on track for ship commands as well. One of them, Lieutenant Commander John Wade of Long Island, New York, left *Benfold* and was immediately given command of a patrol craft, USS *Firebolt. Firebolt* had been run aground under the watch of John's predecessor. By using the *Benfold* playbook, John transformed *Firebolt* in a year from the worst of seven ships in its squadron to the best ship in the squadron. The ship was given the coveted Battle Efficiency Award for its crew's accomplishments.

Another wonderful aspect of great leadership is that you leave a legacy, and your heirs, like John Wade, continue affecting others as they spread throughout the organization.

As the department heads called off their war and focused on purpose, their people started trusting one another more and stopped questioning motives. People started communicating with one another. They helped one another if one department was having a rough time. There were no longer union shops—it was all being done for the collective good. Trust is like a bank account—you have got to keep making deposits if you want it to grow. On occasion, things will go wrong, and you will have to make a withdrawal. Meanwhile, it is sitting in the bank earning interest.

When the entire organization wins, everyone in it wins. No one need be a loser—that construction is bogus.

EVEN THE WORST SCREWUP MAY BE REDEEMABLE.

For career officers, the Navy policy is up or out. You can't stand still: Either you meet promotion standards or you're encouraged to leave. At first glance, this may sound like the right way to trim deadwood and build a strong officer corps, but great talent doesn't always fit the Navy mold. Sometimes the system builds conformity at the expense of competence, and late bloomers are often fired too early. The Navy can't afford those results—it is hard enough just to retain good officers who *do* fit the mold.

Shortly before we left San Diego for the Persian Gulf, my commodore called me to report that our sister ship had fired one of its junior officers as an incompetent. The three-star admiral who ran San Diego told my commodore to find a home for this guy and see if he could be salvaged. We were in desperate need of officers because so many were getting out.

The day before we deployed, *Benfold* received the officer on probation. His name was Elliot, and in short order I discovered that he was among the most gifted naval officers I had ever met. He understood and could recite whole manuals, and could explain complex procedures, such as how to find enemy submarines. He knew more than some of my department heads, yet he was only twenty-three and barely out of the Naval Academy.

Elliot had just one basic problem: He seemed to have little self-confidence, as a consequence of which, he was a magnet for bullies. His previous shipmates had smelled blood and were unmerciful, ridiculing him routinely. The commanding officer didn't help the situation. In my book, nothing is sadder than people who try to inflate themselves by deflating others. The effects on Elliot, though not uncommon, were devastating: In response to being abused, he began to bark at others, perhaps to try to prove to himself that he had some control or power.

I was very blunt with him. I told him that *Benfold*'s crew lived and worked by the Golden Rule. We trusted that everyone would be treated with dignity and respect, and we expected no less for and from him. No one would belittle him, and, of course, he must never ridicule others. And I authorized his chief petty officer to remind Elliot of this conversation if necessary.

By helping him recognize his strengths, we wound up with a winner. Elliot turned out to be one of my best officers. Granted, he took a lot more of my personal time and required more nurturing than others, but my efforts were well invested. When it came to spotting and fighting submarines, for example, no one could match him. Moreover, he learned to take pleasure in helping others recognize their own strengths, instead of the reverse. I was enormously pleased with his contributions and certainly happy to have him, but I was dismayed, if not surprised, that his previous ship had ignored his capabilities.

Elliot eventually qualified as an officer of the deck, which retrieved his career. He went on to another tour in the Navy, then decided to go to business school. He left with his head high, a repaired record, and the confidence that comes from knowing how to lead people, a talent that will reward him enormously as he undertakes his leadership journey.

My work with Elliot produced an unplanned, important benefit. He let me send a crucial signal to the rest of the crew: "You may screw up, but we believe in comebacks. We will help and not give up on you." Leaders and managers need to understand that their employees are keenly attuned to their actions and reactions. If they see you give up on someone, they understand instantly that there's no room for redemption in this outfit, and they could be next to go. If they see you intervene to help someone who is worth your effort, they will be reassured. Though the process is tedious and time-consuming, you will benefit if people feel more secure, are more willing to take risks, and have a positive attitude about the organization. Guess who benefits most? You.

WELCOME THE BAD-NEWS MESSENGER.

It's critical that leaders don't shoot the messenger who brings bad news. A boss who does will not hear about future problems until they are out of hand. It isn't hyperbole to say that it can be a matter of life and death to create a climate of trust in which people are not afraid to deliver news that they know you don't want to hear.

Benfold and other ships like her are incredibly complex structures packed with sophisticated technology, which is upgraded with every advance. Civilian engineers from the companies that built the machines, usually large defense contractors, complete the work. They install the equipment; then we live with the results.

AEGIS is the name of the missile fire control system on ships such as *Benfold*. In Greek mythology, Aegis was the shield made by Zeus from the head of the snake-headed Medusa. Today, it means the "shield of the fleet."

Before we deployed from San Diego, AEGIS engineers installed an upgrade that was supposed to make the system more reliable. In fact, it became less reliable as the numerous power modules within the radar started to short-circuit. When such problems occur, the petty officers on the ship (who are assumed, wrongly, by the contractors not to know how to operate the new equipment) are the first to be blamed.

Since *Benfold* was among the first ships to get the upgrade, and since we discovered the problem before anyone else, the engineers assumed that *we* were the problem. But we started tracking the other upgraded ships and soon learned that they were having the same trouble, but weren't telling anyone about it. I sent an urgent message to my commodore in San Diego telling him that the upgrade was reducing the ships' combat readiness.

I had no idea how he would react, because we had had an odd relationship. When I took command, he had just left for a six-week counternarcotic operation in South America, so I was six weeks into my position before I met him. He called me in when he had to give me my first official fitness report. He rated me sixth out of the six, which didn't surprise me, as I was the most junior of the six. What I wasn't prepared for was that the only substantive thing he wrote was that I was qualified to keep my security clearance. It was a peculiar statement, but I was not upset, because I cared more about results than recognition and I had confidence that results would soon materialize.

I was relieved and delighted that the commodore worked hard to alert everyone who needed to know about the AEGIS problem. When I needed him to tear down barricades on my behalf because our combat readiness was hindered, my boss was totally supportive. AEGIS engineers were called in almost immediately.

You should never bring petty problems to the attention of your boss if you can solve them yourself. But in critical situations like this one, I advise the opposite. Let him or her know as soon as possible. Bad news does not improve with age. The longer you wait, the less time your boss has to help you come up with a solution. The key is to establish your credibility by not being the manager who cries wolf. It was because I never complained about small problems that I was listened to when urgent matters came up. I also did my homework so that when I presented the problem I had all the facts to back up my claims.

Having said that, let me add that a good boss is always a blessing.

Soon after the AEGIS incident, we had a more serious problem. Navy ships have to operate in any climate, from 130-degree heat in the Persian Gulf to below freezing in the North Atlantic. In low temperatures, fuel can jellify, so the ships are equipped with fuel oil service heaters to keep the fuel fluid. Even though

Benfold had yet to operate in cold climates, we were required to keep these heaters operational, just in case.

We were in Singapore for five days of rest and relaxation when, on a routine tour of the engineering plant, one of my sailors noticed fuel dripping from the fuel oil service heater onto a very hot piece of equipment. This was extremely dangerous; the dripping fuel could flash into a major fire that would destroy the entire engine room. We secured fuel throughout the ship and started to investigate. We discovered that the vibration of the ship moving through the water had caused the seals on the service heaters to crack.

I sent messages to my commodore and the admiral immediately, reporting that we had narrowly averted a disaster because of a crewman's alertness. Fearing that this defect could be present on other ships with these same heaters, I recommended that every ship be checked. My commodore wanted to support me, but this was a huge issue, and he wanted to make sure I knew what I was talking about. He sent a message to the commanding officer of a sister ship, which had the same heaters, and asked if he was having the same problem. The commanding officer, an engineer by training, tersely responded that I had vastly overreacted and that he didn't see the need to expend any resources to fix the problem.

To his credit, the commodore didn't accept that answer. He inspected other destroyers of the Arleigh Burke class that happened to be in port, and found that some had the same leaks as *Benfold,* but no one had noticed them yet. Ironically, he even personally inspected our sister ship when she returned to port and found the same problem. He immediately informed the three-star admiral that all Arleigh Burke class destroyers were at risk until the leaks were fixed.

Benfold got kudos for calling attention to this potential disaster. As I have said, you never go wrong when you do the right thing. What gave me the courage to go out on that limb was that my commodore had supported me on the AEGIS problem. Since he had taken me seriously once, I trusted that he would again.

I presented the sailor who discovered the leak with a Navy Achievement Medal right away. Though I should have gone through the bureaucracy for approval, I thought it was more important to make it clear that anyone performing a service for the ship would be recognized immediately. If you wait for the bureaucracy to act, people will forget why they're being recognized in the first place. This kid saved my ship, and I wanted to celebrate him while it was still fresh and made a difference.

This brings up an important point: When do you break the rules?

Bureaucracies can serve useful purposes. For example, a bureaucracy can slow down the implementation of a bad idea by giving the decision-maker more time to reflect. However, more often than not, bureaucracies create rules and then forget why they were needed in the first place, or fail to see that the reasons for them no longer exist.

When it comes to purging outdated regulations, bureaucracies are sclerotic. In today's fast-paced world, rules should be treated as guidelines, not as immutable laws, unless they truly are critical. If the rules weren't critical, I believed that my boss would want me to use my best judgment and do the right thing, regardless of the directive, because there are gray areas.

The gray areas, in fact, are one reason we need mid-level managers. If everything were black and white, organizations would need only chief executives to make the rules and workers to carry them out without questions. Mid-level managers should be the ones to survey the gray areas and provide direction. When I interpreted the rules liberally, I was sure I would not be risking the company if I made an error. When I gave out more medals than I was authorized to do, I was simply using my best judgment to make the best use of the current situation. In the end, the bureaucracy never objected. And if they had objected, the *Washington Post* would have approved, since my decisions were benefiting my people, not me.

PROTECT YOUR PEOPLE FROM
LUNATIC BOSSES.

Some bosses are heartless yet effective, and you have no choice but to endure them until they self-destruct or retire. Others, however, are much worse and should not be tolerated: They are autocrats who verge on lunacy. If power corrupts in civilian life, it can destroy in the military. This happens when someone in authority escapes being accountable and feels omnipotent, and it can endanger everyone. An officer or manager is duty-bound to protect his or her people from someone with this problem.

I recognize fully that shielding your people from such a senior is excruciatingly painful and requires moral courage, but if the danger is clear and present, failure to act is moral cowardice.

For me, this subject is not just academic. During one tour, I worked for two senior officers. One didn't seem to set up his crew for success, even though he ran a good ship, because his leadership style was to demean, and that kept us from being better. Though I wanted to tell him that his behavior was getting him nowhere, I didn't have the courage. The other officer ridiculed his officers and questioned their motives, which destroyed their initiative as well as the unity and purpose we had been working so hard to create.

When it came time for me to stand up and defend these vulnerable officers—well, I stayed seated for fear of getting shot myself. I often look back on that as a squandered opportunity to lead, and am ashamed that I did not provide an asbestos firewall between the captain and his officers.

This is one of the trickiest and most delicate situations a manager can be in. On the one hand, you must support the boss—any company, just like the U.S. Navy, expects loyalty as a condition of employment. On the other hand, you must somehow help to minimize the damage that this behavior will do to the ship's well-being or the company's common interest. There is no easy solution.

Eventually, I learned to manage that officer. I knew what triggered his rage, so whenever I had to deliver bad news, I did it privately, where his ranting and raving would not spew out on others, and I bore the brunt. When someone did exemplary work, I made sure he knew about it; when someone screwed up, I took responsibility for the error. I didn't always succeed in protecting my people. It was a painful time, and I'm not particularly proud of my actions. I could have done more for the junior officers, many of whom left the Navy. However, I did learn a lot about how to deal with impossible bosses. It's a critical skill.

BEING THE BEST CARRIES RESPONSIBILITY.

The price of being the go-to ship is that you often get the toughest jobs, an honor that sometimes feels dubious. *Benfold* had become a key U.S. asset in the Middle East crisis. The Navy considered us so competent with Tomahawk cruise missiles that we were loaded with many more than any other ship. The downside was that we had to stay at sea continuously. Most ships stay out for three weeks at most and then come in for three-day breathers to relax, have a beer, call home. Not us. We had created so much trust in our reliability that we were victims of our own success.

Much later, I heard from a friend in the Pentagon that when our hundred days in the Gulf were finally up, Secretary of Defense William Cohen himself was reported to have asked whether it was advisable to let us leave. He didn't mind rotating two aircraft carriers and a whole fleet of other ships—but *Benfold*, with its cruise missiles, was in a class by itself.

During the height of the crisis, we spent thirty-five straight days at sea. Around day twenty-five, we ran out of things to talk about at dinner. People just ate, got up, looked morose. The monotony left everyone dragging. I began feeling down myself, and when a leader is down the whole organization takes the cue.

I decided I had to buck us all up. I mustered the crew on the flight deck and said a few words: "I know this has been a long haul out here, and that sailors on other ships have been enjoying liberties while you have been working. There's a reason. The Navy considers *Benfold*—and you people are *Benfold*—the most essential ship in the Gulf, the one that can't be spared. Quite simply, we are the best. And being the best carries with it responsibility. Thank you for hanging in there."

Even I was surprised: The crew cheered. They accepted my explanation, and they were proud. Morale turned around dramatically. As I gauged the mood, about 60 percent of the crew were actually disappointed when we finally did pull into port. I grant that some of them were mindful that if you stay out forty-five days you get two free cans of beer, which at that point tastes like champagne, but I think pride was a more important motivation.

That pride took an even greater strain a few weeks later. But it held again, and *Benfold* was rewarded for it.

The big moment had finally arrived. We finished our hundredth day in the Gulf and headed home. Not only had we done great work, we had also escaped any serious injuries or deaths. We hadn't fired any of our Tomahawks in anger, though we had spent several days awaiting launch orders to obliterate sites where Saddam Hussein was producing weapons. Each time when we got down to about five minutes from launch, we were told to hold— the UN secretary-general was again on the verge of negotiating a peace agreement. My crew was deeply disappointed that we did not get to shoot our missiles. There is nothing quite like the adrenaline rush that comes as these extraordinarily powerful weapons are launched. The whole ship shudders and shakes from the blast exhaust. Your heart beats faster as you watch, on closed-circuit television, as these million-dollar swords hurtle out of sight on the journey you made possible. All the hours of training and preparation to do what your country expects of you come together at that very moment. Honor and glory await you—probably even another medal for your chest.

So it was absolutely devastating to have the missiles programmed and battery power applied to them and your finger on the button and then be told, "Never mind." The disappointment was palpable. People were demoralized. It was like when Lucy holds the football for Charlie Brown and then pulls it away at the last minute. Noticing the rapidly spreading dejection around the ship, I knew I had to act quickly or it would be tougher to rally them at the next crisis. They might even start to wonder why we bothered to keep our equipment and skills at peak performance levels if we weren't going to be allowed to use them.

"You have got to act quickly," I thought. I had no idea what to do. In desperate times I always grabbed the microphone to communicate. Your people want to hear it from the top that everything is going to be all right after all. I got on the PA system and told them that I understood their disappointment, but we were on station and prepared. We had forced Saddam back to the bargaining table. So we had actually succeeded in our mission. Due to the crew's professionalism, we had maintained peace. Guess what? The mood shifted back. My crew was back to brimming with pride and esprit de corps because they had done what they were supposed to do. In times of peril, people always turn to the guy at the top and look for guidance. In fact, one of the least-understood aspects of our Navy is that, on any given day, more than 50 percent of our ships are at sea, whether on station maintaining this deterrent or preparing and sharpening our skills so that we will be ready when needed.

As we all know, an agreement with Saddam was never finalized. But our presence and readiness forced him to negotiate. Truth be told, I was secretly glad that we were not told to fire. For all their accuracy and reliability, those missiles could drift off course and kill innocent civilians—a possibility I found very sobering.

At 0755 on the morning of January 2, 1998, we weighed anchor off Bahrain for the voyage home. The whole crew was happily focused on our first scheduled stop: Australia, a country that welcomes American sailors perhaps more warmly than any other place on earth. The fact that we had not been allowed to shoot was now a distant memory. Everyone was excited. I had even lined up fleet oilers to refuel us at sea so we could make the trip nonstop, a very unusual occurrence these days due to budget cutbacks.

But no sooner had the anchor chain been secured than I got a call from the commodore in charge of search-and-seizure operations in the Gulf, Commodore Mike Duffy. That Duffy was difficult was something upon which other commanding officers agreed. Yet I came to understand him. He was extraordinarily demanding and held you accountable for your performance. Over the course of one hundred days, he had come to love *Benfold* because we provided results. It was the ships that didn't that hated him.

I knew right away: *Benfold* was being drafted for yet another go-to job. Hold the shrimp, hold the barbie. Do not pass go. Do not collect $200. At this point, I was actually wishing that we were not so good, so we could rest.

"A ship smuggling contraband is headed down the Iranian coast," the commodore said. "I have run out of spare ships to track it. Can you take charge?"

Everyone on the *Benfold* bridge heard the call, because the radio speakers were turned on. They all looked at me. I believe the F-word passed my lips. Some witnesses would later say that I said it multiple times (out of deference to my mother, I need to let the record show that I did not learn that language at home). We had given at the office, and now we were being asked to give yet again. It wasn't fair—especially when you consider that the other two ships, *Gary* and *Harry W. Hill,* which together hadn't made a tenth of our contribution, were merrily on their way to Australia.

"Commodore," I said, "*Benfold* is your ship. We will do it." My crew's hearts sank. There was no joy in Mudville.

"This should take only two days, maybe less," the commodore said. "What speed will you need to make up the lost time getting to Australia?"

Our normal transit speed was sixteen knots to save fuel; only one engine was needed at that speed. Just off the top of my head, I said twenty-four knots, which would require two engines burning twice the fuel.

"I guarantee you will get extra fuel for your twenty-four knots." That assurance meant that the commodore was going out on a limb to take care of us. At that moment, Mike Duffy was my hero.

The crew cheered. I smiled. I knew that if I had put up any resistance, Duffy would not have given us the extra fuel.

We put to sea and chased the smuggler down the Iranian coast. Soon a British warship joined us, but the rogue ship managed to skip into Dubai waters, where we were banned from picking up smugglers. We could have stopped it by firing warning shots, but there were too many other fishing boats around and I didn't want to risk killing innocent civilians. I asked the commodore for a helicopter to help chase the smuggler, but the only one available was parked on the *Gary*—which initially declined to share it because the ship was en route to Australia. I thought it likely that the copter could have caught up with the ship after helping us, without significantly delaying the *Gary*. Commodore Duffy commandeered the aircraft by tersely ordering *Gary*'s CO to lend it to us.

I felt all the better for having taken on the chase mission without sniffling, no matter how reluctant I felt at the time, even though it was ultimately an unsuccessful mission. Helping your boss when he or she needs you badly is a pretty good investment.

We finally set out across the Indian Ocean on January 3, only a day behind schedule, and checked into Fremantle in Western Australia on January 11. Our orders called for ten days of port visits in the wonderful Land of Oz, but I guessed that no one would be checking our track, so I stepped on the gas between ports, and we squeezed out twelve days ashore. We wasted a few taxpayer dollars on excess fuel, but the return on investment in terms of crew morale more than covered the cost.

TRUST ALSO MAKES MONEY.

Back in 1994, when I was second in command of *Shiloh,* some friends and I went out to eat at a restaurant on Coronado Island, across the bay from San Diego. As we sat at the bar waiting for our table, I struck up a conversation with an older gentleman by the name of Irv Refkin. It turned out that his wife of forty-seven years had just died, and he was very lonely. I invited him to join us for dinner. We have been good friends ever since.

In 1997, when I was back in San Diego getting ready to take command of *Benfold,* Irv and I went out to dinner once or twice a month. He owned a repair shop with about seventy-five employees. The company did repairs on Navy ships as well as some commercial work on pumps, motors, circuit breakers, and the like. It was a very successful specialty shop.

I asked Irv what his business philosophy was. He said he preferred a handshake to a contract, he treasured his reputation, and he treated his employees with respect and dignity. He summed up: "Trust makes money."

I asked for an example. "Time clocks," he answered. He described how he had installed time clocks for his employees back when they were all the rage. Then he had second thoughts. Didn't they imply a lack of trust? Out went the time clocks. As a result, his people not only worked full days without fail, but most worked longer than eight hours—they felt trusted.

Next, Irv moved on to tools. His general manager told him they needed a tool-issue room to make sure employees did not steal the tools. So Irv hired a tool-issue custodian for about $35,000 a year. He went down one morning and found a long line of employees waiting to check out tools. In the evening, there was another line to return them. This lack of trust was costing him money. So he did away with the tool-issue room, reassigned the custodian to other work, and the following year he had to spend only $2,000 for tools that were stolen or lost. Once again, trust was a moneymaker.

His trust extended to customers as well—and it was reciprocated. If an admiral needed something repaired immediately, Irv dispensed with negotiations and contracts and got to work. His shop became the go-to shop on the waterfront when you wanted something fixed right the first time, at a good price, and without any hassle.

My Irv Refkin story doesn't stop there. After taking command of *Benfold*, I invited him aboard for a tour. My sailors were loading food. It comes in big boxes, and you form a human chain to pass them from the pier to the ship and down into the storage compartments. It is very hard work, and people can be injured. This was the first time Irv had seen the operation. "After 225 years in business," he said, "you'd think the Navy could figure out a better method."

Irv went back to his shop and told one of his people to design a conveyer belt that could load the boxes automatically. A couple of weeks later, the prototype was finished. The bottom line: Irv now has a Navy contract to load stores on ships via a conveyor belt.

He would have preferred a handshake agreement, of course, but they made him put it in writing. Navy trust hasn't caught up with Irv quite yet.

CHAPTER SIX

LOOK FOR RESULTS, NOT SALUTES

LIKE MILITARY SERVICES AROUND THE GLOBE, THE U.S. Navy is a hierarchy. Rank, seniority, and military discipline govern nearly everything. "Officer Country" signs ban enlisted people from parts of nearly every ship.

As gently as possible, I set out to chip away at this rigid system. Formal etiquette is never out of style in the Navy, nor was it on my ship. When I walked on deck, sailors cleared gangways, threw salutes, and stood at attention facing me, backs to bulkheads. They were honoring the office, as sailors must. But in a short time they learned that I was not interested in flattery or fluff. Rigidity gets in the way of creativity. Instead of salutes, I wanted results, which to me meant achieving combat readiness. The way to accomplish this was not to order it from the top, which is demoralizing and squashes initiative. I wanted sailors to open their minds, use their imaginations, and find better ways of doing everything. I wanted officers to understand that ideas and initiative could emerge from the lower deck as well as muscle and blind obedience. And I wanted everyone on the ship to see one another as people and shipmates.

As captain, I was charged with enforcing 225 years of accumulated Navy regulations, policies, and procedures. But every last one of those rules was up for negotiation whenever my people came up with a better way of doing things. As soon as one of their new ideas worked in practice, I passed it up the chain of command, hoping my superiors would share it with other ships.

To facilitate that, I had to encourage the crew to take initiative—and make sure the officers welcomed it. And that meant they would have to get to know one another as people. They would have to respect one another, and from that would come trust.

HELP KNOCK DOWN THE BARRIERS.

On Sunday afternoons when the ship was at sea, we had cookouts on the aft flight deck, which was otherwise used for the antisubmarine helicopter. One Sunday early in my command, I went back to observe the cookout. A long line of sailors stood waiting to get their lunch. My officers would cut to the head of the line to get their food, and then go up to the next deck to eat by themselves. The officers weren't bad people; they just didn't know any different. It's always been that way.

When I saw this, I decided to go to the end of the line. The officers were looking down, curious. They elected the supply officer to come talk to me.

"Captain," he said, looking worried, "you don't understand. You go to the head of the line."

"That's okay," I said. "If we run out of food, I will be the one to go without."

I stood in line and got my food. Then I stayed on the lower deck and ate with the sailors. The officers became totally alert. You could almost hear the gears shifting in their heads.

The next weekend we had another cookout, and, without my saying anything to anyone, the officers went to the end of the line. When they got their lunch, they stayed on the lower level and mingled with the sailors. Given the Navy's basically classist society, to say that the fraternal scene on the flight deck was unusual would be an understatement. To me, it felt right.

Within a month after taking command, I felt I was making progress in proving to my crew that I genuinely cared about them and would work with them to develop their potential. But the crew knew that a captain has to answer to those above in the chain of command, and I knew my sailors were waiting to see how I would act within the larger context of the Navy. Did innovation and empowerment end at *Benfold*'s gangway?

In mid-July 1997, I got a chance to show them. We were engaged in a weeklong exercise to get ready for the Persian Gulf. Again *Benfold* was traveling with *Gary* and *Harry W. Hill*. The senior officer in charge of this exercise, a commodore embarked on

Hill, was not particularly creative, but I considered him a nice guy and a solid officer.

When the exercise started, I was down in the combat information center, where the ship-to-ship radio blared continuous calls from the commodore and other officers on *Gary* and *Hill*. And I soon realized that I was the only person answering. When I asked for an explanation, I was told that because so many people had previously been verbally chastised if they erred, no one would now take the initiative. This climate actually is very dangerous. In combat, you can have as many as ten radios needing attention and passing critical information at the same time, and obviously no one person can handle that. I authorized everyone to answer calls and make the necessary decisions, which surprised people who had never been given this level of responsibility.

Halfway through the exercise, the commodore flew over for a routine visit to see how things were going and gauge the morale of my crew. He flew in at 1100 hours, and we sat in my stateroom for half an hour. The plan was for him to stay for lunch, and at 1130 he headed for the officers' wardroom.

"Commodore," I said, "that's not where we're having lunch."

He looked at me quizzically and asked what I had in mind. I told him we were dining on the enlisted mess decks with my crew. His eyes grew wide. "I have not eaten a meal on the mess decks in years," he said.

"Yes sir," I said, "but I'd like you to meet my crew, talk to my sailors. They might have questions for you."

Crews complain when a senior officer or VIP is scheduled to come aboard and they're ordered to clean or even paint the ship in preparation, but have to be out of sight when the eminence arrives—as though they're not good enough to mingle with the brass.

Well, on my ship, the VIPs *were* my crew, and I wanted the senior officers to spend time with them so they could discover how truly talented and dedicated they are. I wanted the brass to start developing the same respect for our people that I had. I escorted the commodore to the mess decks and straight to the end of the line, where we stood waiting like everyone else. Of course, my sailors spoke to him respectfully, but, as they had already learned with me, quite freely. They were having an ordinary conversation with an esteemed colleague. The commodore had never had this experience before, and to his credit, he loved it.

After we filled our trays, we found seats at two separate tables. Now the commodore was on his own with seven sailors. They asked good questions; he listened intently and answered directly. I could see from my own table that everyone was interested, involved, smiling, and having fun, which for me was both gratifying and something of a relief. If the commodore had been a traditional martinet, the experiment could easily have been a fiasco.

Instead, he was impressed by the caliber of my crew's questions. He had had no idea that lesser ranks could teach him anything. But when one petty officer asked him what he thought about the Navy's "leadership continuum," a new training program for enlisted people, the commodore was caught short: He knew nothing about it. Since the program affected only enlisted people, not officers, he had seen no reason to pay attention to it. Now he realized, with a shock, that he was totally ignorant about a program of vital importance to 1,500 sailors aboard the six ships under his command. Another boss might have been resentful at being shown up, but again, I had gauged him right.

When we left the mess decks and returned to my cabin, he said this had been the most worthwhile experience he'd ever had in the Navy. From now on he planned to have lunch on the mess decks of whatever ship he visited. To my knowledge, he has kept that promise, and as a result has stayed in close touch with what crews think, need, and want.

From that incident forward, I resolved that VIPs would always eat with my crew. And if the VIP wasn't around at mealtime, I would make sure that he or she had other opportunities to interact with the crew.

I started eating at least one meal per week on the mess decks with the crew. It paid big dividends; I learned a great deal and got to know people that way, and after a while my officers began taking occasional meals there, too. I usually went to the noon meal on Wednesdays, and it's a Navy tradition that lunch on Wednesday is always cheeseburgers. (The Navy term for them is "sliders," in tribute to the grease.) Well, my senior enlisted advisor, Command Master Chief Bob Scheeler, of Laramie, Wyoming, was a huge "Parrot Head," a fan of the singer Jimmy Buffett. So every Wednesday at precisely 1130, we would play Buffett's "Cheeseburger in Paradise" over the public-address system. It was cool at first; then everyone got sick of it—except Bob. He continued to play it. We finally got *so* sick of it that it became cool again. But on the last Wednesday of our deployment to the Persian Gulf, I decided that that song would play no more on my ship. So we had a raffle for charity. A one-dollar contribution bought you a chance to shoot the CD with a shotgun. We raised over $1,000 for charity and never again played that song—until my last Wednesday in command of *Benfold*.

As a result of his tour on *Benfold*, Master Chief Scheeler is an icon in the enlisted ranks. Sailors and master chief petty officers alike want to know how he blossomed as a genuine leader during the time we worked together. I recently asked him what he tells other command master chiefs when they ask what made the biggest difference for him as a leader, and his response amazed me. I had completely forgotten the incident that he never will.

The position of command master chief has the potential to be either the best job in the Navy or the worst. It entails representing the interests of the enlisted population to the upper ranks on the ship. Master Chief Scheeler often told me that he previously had felt like his views were ignored.

I felt his views deserved attention. Our meetings on the ship were usually held in the officers' mess, which had seats for only fifteen people. More than that attended, so many stood. It was standing room only at my first meeting after taking command. I had a reserved seat, as did my XO. I took a look around the room and saw that Master Chief Scheeler was standing three deep in the back of the room. Without clearly thinking through the ramifications of what I was about to say, I announced that from then on, the command master chief of USS *Benfold*, like the CO and XO, would have a reserved seat. His would be to my immediate left, and the XO would be to my right. The department head who had to vacate the seat flashed a look indicating that he was clearly perturbed. But as I intended, the enlisted crew realized that Master Chief Scheeler now had prominence, and that the needs of the entire crew would be taken into consideration.

Master Chief Scheeler was now going to play a critical role in charting the course on *Benfold*. Sometimes all you need is a seat at the table. From that day forward, Scheeler never let me or his people down. He has become a sought-after sage for his knowledge about leadership.

The Arleigh Burke class of destroyers, which includes *Benfold*, is named after a World War II commodore who won the battle of Cape St. George with a squadron that was undermanned and outgunned by the Japanese. Admiral Arleigh Burke, a certified naval hero, went on to become chief of naval operations, and he commissioned a painting of his ships going into the battle. It was a splendid picture. Shortly before his death at age ninety-eight, he gave the first of 750 prints of it to Defense Secretary Perry. One day I came home from sea to find a huge package on my front porch; it was the painting. Perry had sent it to me. I think Perry had seen my face when I first saw that painting. It would have looked wonderful on my stateroom wall, where I could have enjoyed it every day, but I wanted the crew to be reminded at every meal of the ship's history and tradition stretching all the way back to World War II. So I had it displayed on the mess decks, and I think they really appreciated it.

LET YOUR CREW FEEL FREE TO SPEAK UP.

I was determined to create a culture where everyone on board felt comfortable enough to say to me, "Captain, have you thought of this?" or "Captain, I'm worried about something," or even "Captain, I think you're dead wrong and here's why." Yes-people are a cancer in any organization, and dangerous to boot.

Throughout my career, I have watched people at the top actively discourage lower ranks from speaking up and contributing all that they can. On one ship I served in, we got a new executive officer. He was very talented; we would have felt comfortable going to war under his command. But his major flaw was that you could not tell him anything. He knew it all, period.

We were at sea one morning at 0530, before reveille had sounded, when he hit the deck running and ordered a man-overboard drill. That's a crucial test of the crew's readiness to save a downed pilot, help another vessel in distress, or rescue a crew member in heavy weather. It requires precise seamanship by everyone from the officer of the deck to the coxswain guiding the small boat that will pick up the man overboard. It's a great exercise when done properly, and it boosts morale—not only by helping everyone improve his or her skills, but also by reassuring sailors that if they were washed into the sea, their buddies could save them.

The XO was so gung-ho that he chose to sound the alarm before reveille and wake everyone from a deep sleep. There was nothing wrong with that, because this was just an exercise in safe waters off the coast of California. Had we been part of a carrier battle group in an actual search for submarines, we would have been towing decoys astern on a cable about six hundred feet long. In that situation, if any enemy sub fired a torpedo at the ship, you can activate noisemakers on the decoys that fool the torpedo into heading for them instead of your ship.

The problem was that these decoys made it impossible to change course more than 180 degrees at one time, because the propellers would run over the cables and cut them. Man-overboard drills require a tight, full circle to get the ship back to its original position in the line. Clearly, something had to give.

I was standing watch in the ship's combat information center, and as soon as I heard that the drill had been launched, I asked the XO to give me fifteen minutes to reel in the decoys. But he wanted to proceed with the exercise without delay. The next thing I knew, a floating dummy was tossed overboard, the whistle sounded six short blasts to signal a man overboard, all four engines accelerated to thirty knots, and the ship turned sharply, heading straight for the decoys. I got on the PA system and warned the XO three times about the cables. "Reel them in, reel them in; I'm proceeding with this exercise," he shouted. But I couldn't reel them in in less than fifteen minutes; the drill was going to be over in four. The third time I tried to warn him, the XO called back, "Don't tell me again, I know they're out there. Reel them in."

The operation was a spectacular success, but the patient died. The severed decoy cables cost the taxpayers some $50,000. Moreover, it took almost three months to replace the cables, during which time, had we been attacked by torpedoes, we could not have distracted them as effectively. In short, we could have coordinated better with each other.

I wish I could say that the need to improve listening skills and less-than-perfect coordination happened only in the past. But the tragic sinking of a Japanese fishing boat off Honolulu by the submarine USS *Greeneville* suggests otherwise. The moment I heard about it, I was reminded that, as is often the case with accidents, someone senses possible danger but doesn't necessarily speak up. As the *Greeneville* investigation unfolded, I read in a *New York Times* article that the submarine's crew "respected the commanding officer too much to question his judgment." If that's respect, then I want none of it. You need to have people in your organization that can tap you on your shoulder and say, "Is this the best way?" or "Slow down," or "Think about this," or "Is what we are doing worth killing or injuring somebody?"

History records countless incidents in which ship captains or organization managers permitted a climate of intimidation to pervade the workplace, silencing subordinates whose warnings could have prevented disaster. Even when the reluctance to speak up stems from admiration for the commanding officer's skill and experience, a climate to question decisions must be created in order to foster double-checking.

Make your people feel they can speak freely, no matter what they want to say. If they see that the captain wears no clothes, let them say so; facts are facts and deserve attention, not retribution. Yes, I'm pushing you to work harder at leading your organization. Yes, the climate I prescribe is tough to create. But in my view, had someone been comfortable tapping that commanding officer and saying, "Sticking to a schedule isn't important enough to justify taking safety shortcuts," that accident on *Greeneville* might have been avoided. How they all must wish they had that day to live over.

When leaders and managers behave as though they are above their people, when they announce decisions after little or no consultation, when they make it clear that their orders aren't to be questioned, then conditions are ripe for disaster. The good news is that every leader has the power to prevent this. Once leadership opportunities are squandered, you can never get them back. Don't live your life with regrets.

FREE YOUR CREW FROM TOP-DOWN-ITIS.

The fall of 1997 was a heady time aboard *Benfold*. The ship was improving, and morale was soaring. Still, I was determined to turn the ship into an institution of continual learning, which entailed a systematic and methodical analysis of what worked and what didn't.

At first my ambition seemed quixotic. I remember sitting in my captain's chair on the bridge, watching some sailors screw up a simple operation on the deck below, gripping the chair arms until my knuckles turned white. My sailors were painting some fittings on the fire stations bright red. The only problem was, they weren't using a drop cloth, and red paint was dripping all over the gray deck that they had painted only a week before. Now they would have to go back and repaint the deck gray. What was wrong with those people? Why couldn't they see that they were creating more work for themselves? But instead of flaring up like Captain Bligh, threatening to draw and quarter every dummy who disgraced my ship, I bit my tongue.

The incident induced a memory from my childhood. Every summer, I had to paint the trim—on our brick house one year, the garage the next. One time I, too, failed to use a drop cloth and dripped white paint on the red brick. My mother tore a huge chunk from my behind (she hadn't yet learned the art of grassroots leadership either), which taught me the lesson, but left me mad and resentful. So I explained to my sailors how using a drop cloth would directly benefit their free time, and they got the message.

And slowly, as they warmed to the new approach, the crew began to take responsibility for their mistakes.

I wanted them to "own" *Benfold*, to feel that it was their ship, and to turn it into the fittest ship in the Pacific Fleet.

Of course, I treated people with the same dignity and respect I expected from them, and I made sure they truly liked their jobs. Freed from top-down-itis, *Benfold*'s sailors were given responsibilities to make decisions, correct mistakes, and prove to themselves that they were part of a superb crew.

I anticipated some short-term problems. I knew our performance could dip a bit as people were learning and growing comfortable with their new responsibilities. I also knew that the admirals could interpret this as *Benfold*'s decline under my command. Still, I wanted to leave the Navy a legacy, and I was prepared never to be promoted again if that was the price I had to pay. My crew was going to be trained to make decisions. Few skills are more vital or would benefit them and their organizations more than that one, no matter where life took them.

NURTURE THE FREEDOM TO FAIL.

I worked hard to create a climate that encouraged quixotic pursuits and celebrated the freedom to fail. I never once reprimanded a sailor for attempting to solve a problem or reach a goal. I wanted my people to feel empowered, so they could think autonomously. In the business community today, "empowerment" seems to be a four-letter word, but that's because it is misunderstood to mean letting your people do whatever they want. Empower your people, and at the same time give them guidelines within which they are allowed to roam. I called it my line in the sand: I had to be in on any decision that could kill someone, injure someone, waste taxpayers' money, or damage the ship. But short of that, anyone on my ship should try to solve any problem that came up. Trying takes grit, builds skills, breeds courage.

Before we left for the Persian Gulf, a chief petty officer from the Australian navy was assigned to *Benfold* for six months. He was a big rugby fan, a game my sailors had never played but were happy to learn. He started a rugby clinic, and eventually we had a *Benfold* rugby team. We bought uniforms that made us the best-looking rugby team in the U.S. Navy (of course, we were the only rugby team in the U.S. Navy). Unfortunately, we had to leave for the Gulf soon after the team was assembled, so their skills stagnated. As for actual talent, well, let's just say they weren't World Cup quality.

When we finally pulled into port, the *Benfold* team challenged the International Rugby Team of Dubai. That took some gall: Dubai is full of expatriate Brits who take rugby very seriously. My sailors had a lot of spirit, but they had been at sea for thirty-five straight days, their stamina was shaky, and they lacked talent to begin with. So we got slaughtered, 77 to 4. It was pitiful. Worse, rugby is a very rough game with a high body count. Some of my star sailors were out there getting crunched, and I could just see them winding up with blown knees or broken legs, having to be flown back to the United States, leaving *Benfold* shorthanded.

To my amazement, not one player was injured during the whole game. We had just one casualty—a young ensign who had flown in from stateside that very day and was sitting in the stands watching the game. As she looked away for a moment, the rugby ball sailed off the field and hit her left pinky, completely dislocating it. The pain was bad enough, but far worse was that she was a concert pianist with plans for a music career.

We rushed her to the American International Hospital in Dubai, where they put her finger back into place. Fortunately, she had a full recovery. How mysterious, though, that with all those bodies crashing into one another on the rugby field, the sole person injured was a concert pianist sitting in the stands. Someone up there really did love my crew. It was probably Edward Benfold.

So we were slaughtered out there on the playing field. Who cares? I was thrilled that they had felt confident enough to take on the more experienced team. All managers should nurture the freedom to fail.

INNOVATION KNOWS NO RANK.

In business terms, I viewed *Benfold* during its Persian Gulf deployment as a very productive company with one major customer—my boss, the three-star admiral in command of the Fifth Fleet. To dominate market share, our ship had to top all others in the categories most important to my customer. Given his relatively scarce resources—too few ships to handle constantly increasing U.S. commitments in the region—we focused on two ways we could help him most and beat our competitors in the process.

The first way was to achieve perfect marksmanship with Tomahawk missiles. Since we had practiced all the way across the western Pacific, we aced this exercise, performing better than any other ship stationed in the Gulf. As a result, the three-star gave us more cruise missiles (more than double our original allocation), making us the biggest arsenal in the fleet. It was a distinct honor.

Our second big opportunity for customer service involved the

United Nations inspections of all ships entering and leaving Iraq. The admiral was responsible for making sure that no embargoed oil was smuggled out and no prohibited materials got in. It was and still is a difficult and tedious job. Navy ships boarded every ship traveling in the area, performed a thorough inspection, and sent the clean ones rapidly on their way. As in all transport business, time was money, so we had to avoid needless delays that might cost some company millions and inflame anti-U.S. sentiment in the region.

At one point, when bad weather prevented our boarding, we were forced to make five Iraq-bound tankers wait at anchor for three days. When the weather improved, Commodore Duffy ordered us to clear the ships as quickly as possible, as he was taking heat for the delays. We had them pull into a tight circle with *Benfold* in the center and sent out two search teams. We cleared the five ships—including all paperwork—in two and a half hours. That was a record.

The commodore phoned me right away: "This can't be. Are you sure you thoroughly boarded those ships?"

"Absolutely."

"I'm coming over to observe you next time."

"Aye-aye, sir. Please do."

I could afford to be serene, even smug. Thanks to a junior petty officer, Fire Controlman Derrick Thomas, *Benfold* had found a shortcut.

The boarding paperwork, required by the United Nations, was excruciatingly time-consuming and tedious, consisting of more than a hundred questions. Worse, half of them had to be answered in radio conversations with the shipmasters, most of whom spoke very poor English. Compiling the entire written report could take days.

After watching our officers suffer through this process in an earlier boarding, Petty Officer Thomas spoke up: "Why not create a database and speed this up? A lot of ships make this trip every week."

I was on the bridge at the time. My officers looked at him and looked away. I would not have traded any of my officers for any others in the Navy. They were sharp. They were energetic. They knew their stuff. But as I said before, they were trained not to listen to the crew. Thomas was so junior they barely even acknowledged his existence. So I asked him to elaborate.

"We have got electronic access to all these reports for the last year on every ship that's come in and gone out," he said. "Of the hundred items on the list of questions, fifty or sixty are routine information that never changes from trip to trip. I can create a database on the routine stuff, so that even before you call a ship to stop, you will have 50 percent of the information you need up here on your laptop screen. You don't have to keep asking and translating over and over. The whole job, including the written reports, will take half the time."

I told him to construct the database. It included more than 150 ships that had previously been boarded. Suddenly, we had half the report done before our search party went aboard, which explains how we cleared the five weather-delayed tankers and completed the written report in two and a half hours.

At our next boarding, Commodore Duffy came over on a helicopter. He was impressed by the efficiency of our search-and-seizure team, but he was astounded by the computerized database.

"We have been boarding ships in the Gulf for the past six years," he said, "and no one ever came up with the idea to catalog all this information. Congratulations. Make me a copy right away."

Our database was promptly distributed to every other Navy ship performing boarding duties in the Gulf—and it's still being used.

Obviously, the prime lesson of this story is that good ideas are where you find them—even on the fo'c'sle. My officers were ready to discard a great idea because it came from a lowly enlisted man. Fortunately, I happened to overhear his recommendation. Every leader needs big ears and zero tolerance for stereotypes. But I will digress to point out two other lessons that may bear on your company:

1. With too few ships to inspect too many tankers, the admiral needed big results from limited resources. That's a problem many organizations share. Multitasking with the assets at your disposal is the only way to solve it. *Benfold* mastered the art of multitasking.
2. By getting very good at both inspecting tankers and shooting cruise missiles, *Benfold* achieved two coveted areas of expertise. The higher-ups were forever fighting over who got to use our services. That should be the goal of any business: Strive to offer high quality at low cost in versatile areas such that customers fight to place their orders.

CHALLENGE YOUR CREW BEYOND ITS REACH.

Around the same time that stainless steel fasteners came into my life, I asked another sailor what he thought of our training program.

"To be honest," he answered, "it's not all that good. You hand us the Navy training manual and make us order every item off the menu. You have never once asked the trainees what we feel we need."

"Good point," I said. Inwardly, I could not help wondering how a chief boatswain's mate or a Marine drill instructor would react to this complaint. Ask recruits what they "feel" they need? You must be kidding. Recruits are forbidden to feel anything; they do what chiefs and sergeants are paid to tell them to do.

Even so, I put together a team of trainers and trainees, and we completely revised our training program.

Training is the lifeblood of the Navy. In any given year, you lose about one-third of your crew to transfers, discharges, injuries, or retirements. So the job of training never ends, and worse, you never get it quite right. In my eighteen-year career, I found Navy training generally inefficient and all too prone to incite discontent, if not outright loathing. If we ever did a return-on-investment study on training in the military, heads would roll.

After a ship returns to its home port and completes a nine-week maintenance period, it begins the training needed to certify its readiness for the next deployment. After our Gulf service, *Benfold* began this process. It was soon after the Navy had revamped its training system to make it more responsive to today's demands. The new version hit the usual resistance to change, but on *Benfold* we thought it was a quantum improvement—and with our trademark hubris, we considered it well worth trying to improve it even more. Of course, we had no inkling of how much effort lay ahead.

The premise of the old training system was that all hands must be raised to the same skill level. But there was no flexibility in the group lessons. Even if eight out of ten people achieved perfection, the exercise had to be repeated until the two laggards caught up. You can imagine how all this repetition tended to vaporize time, not to mention interest and morale.

Our solution was simple. We used technology to leverage our training time. We made our training tougher than anything we would ever see in combat. And we picked up the part of the new system that allowed targeted training for laggards. If two people were weak, they got remedial training apart from the other eight, which obviously saved time and presumably strengthened their confidence and skills.

But as good as all this sounds in theory, in practice it was a mess. The problem was that the data-recording process had not kept pace with technology. Records of which sailors completed which exercise, and when, were recorded with paper and pencils. Yes, you read that correctly: paper and pencils.

This antediluvian absurdity was sabotaging the new program: It snarled the scheduling, and ship after ship failed the final exam. The program's critics bad-mouthed it, and the commodore in charge, who strongly believed in it, found himself dangling from a yardarm.

Believe it or not—and by now you probably believe it—no one had ever thought to computerize the records. So we did just that.

The petty officer who had created the Persian Gulf database, Derrick Thomas, now made another one. Hit a key and you could see the training results: dates, scores, laggards, stars. The program even scheduled the training sessions. It was a phenomenal leap forward, ensuring snarl-free training and focusing on whomever needed special attention.

Once that database was in place, we could use another powerful tool. The new technology embedded in ships allows captains to build their own training scenarios, tailored to all the possible places they can be expected to do battle. I programmed into our computer all of the possible forces that Iraq could throw at us; then I was able to build a simulated battle to test my crew's skill in combating those threats. I could tailor these battles to any expected threat, anywhere in the world. In fact, I made the scrimmage tougher than anything we would ever see in real life. Some ships never took advantage of this breakthrough.

When we arrived in San Diego, we faced a weeklong assessment, a sort of mini-Olympics of Navy training. We had publicly stated that our goal was to validate the entire training program. This immodest assertion drove the old dinosaurs up the wall. They thought no one could be that good. Some even visited our ship during the assessment, all primed to see us eat our words.

But we were ready. During the first week, assessors came aboard to evaluate the crew's level of training and assign us the final challenge that we would have to master before we could graduate, which Navy precedent said would be six months later.

I'm sure you will forgive my pride when I tell you that *Benfold* aced the final graduation challenge at week one of the six-month process. We also got the highest score ever—higher than any ship that trained for the entire six months. How did we do it? The sailors themselves had redesigned the training program and made it more effective than the Navy had ever dreamed.

I called the commodore. "Sir," I said, straining to sound humble, "we just passed the training, and therefore don't have to go to sea for the six months of training."

There was a pause while he picked up his jaw. "We're not set up to do that," he said finally. "You have to go to sea for six months."

I gently negotiated with him. There's an art to managing your boss, and all bosses can be managed if you know what their triggers are. A universal trigger is saving money. So I explained that the commodore could save bundles in fuel costs if he let us modify our training schedule and spend much less time at sea, since our readiness was already the best. He could use that fuel on the ships whose proficiency was not up to our level. He finally agreed to a two-month training program. My crew had saved themselves four months of hard work. But when I proudly gave them the news, one sailor raised his hand: "This is free time, right?"

"Sure."

"Why don't we go on port visits?"

"No ships ever go on port visits during this training process," I said. "But I will ask."

I called the commodore. "No ships ever go on port visits during this training process," he told me.

"Why not?"

There was another one of his long pauses. "Well," he said, "I guess there's really no good reason why not."

So for the next two months, we cruised the coast, making port visits at Puerto Vallarta and Cabo San Lucas in Mexico, San Francisco, and Victoria, Canada. My sailors were in hog heaven—and they had earned it.

CHAPTER SEVEN

TAKE CALCULATED RISKS

THE U.S. NAVY IS NO MORE FOND OF PEOPLE WHO GO out on a limb than is any other bureaucracy. In fact, taking a risk is seen as a danger to your career. But an organization that aims to stay alive and strong should make sure to praise and promote risk-takers, even if they fail once in a while. Unfortunately, organizations all too often promote only those who have never made a mistake. Show me someone who has never made a mistake, and I will show you someone who is not doing anything to improve your organization.

As I have said, I never took a reckless risk in my Navy career. Each danger I ran was a calculated part of my campaign to create change without asking permission from higher authority. I took only the risks that I thought my boss would want me to take, risks I could defend within my job description and authority. For the most part, they produced beneficial results, and my boss got the credit for that, so he didn't object.

Still, some risks are more dangerous than others. In general:

BET ON THE PEOPLE WHO THINK FOR THEMSELVES.

When I took command of *Benfold*, I saw a crew of 310 men and women with untapped talent, untested spirit, and unlimited potential. I was determined to be the captain these sailors deserved.

I wanted to send a loud message that would prove I was serious about making them partners, not peons. But I knew that words alone would have little impact. They had heard all the Navy slogans a thousand times. Every admiral says our people come first, but few back those words with actions. What I needed was a dramatic gesture. Fortunately, an opportunity came four days after I took command, when we faced the challenging job of refueling at sea.

Navy ships carry at least half a tank of fuel at all times (*Benfold*'s tanks hold almost 500,000 gallons). This keeps them ready for emergencies. If you're called on to help another vessel in distress, for example, you might have to travel great distances with no access to filling stations. When you get down to half a tank, you're supposed to refuel. And that job gets exciting when you do it at sea.

Refueling at sea involves navigating alongside an oiler—a Navy tanker that carries some eight million gallons of fuel. The ships stay parallel, moving ahead steadily at about fifteen knots—sixteen and a half miles an hour. After you maneuver your ship to a distance of 120 feet from the tanker, the tanker's crew sends over two cables, each carrying an eight-inch fuel hose. The cables are tensioned so that they will remain taut when the two ships separate or converge by a few yards, but the margin of error is thin. You always worry about breaking the lines by veering too far apart or dipping the hoses into the sea, ripping them away, if the ships get too close together. You hook the hoses to your tanks for the refill, and you can probably pump 200,000 gallons in a little over an hour and a half.

Refueling at sea is great fun but also very dangerous, especially in rough seas; the two ships are in danger of crashing into each other, risking structural damage as well as explosions. The job requires expert ship handling, and officers put their careers on the line every time they do it. It's crucial to practice often so that you become proficient, and also to make sure that when your junior officers become commanders, they won't be afraid of refueling their ships.

By all accounts, *Benfold* had not refueled much at sea. Most of the previous refuelings had been done at the pier in port, which was not as dangerous. When I took command of *Benfold,* we had less than half a tank. So within days I ordered up a refueling at sea. I was now responsible for the ship and did not want to be caught unprepared.

Only the combat systems officer, Lieutenant Kevin Hill, was thoroughly proficient with the maneuver. Though he was outstanding at it, no ship or company can rely on just one person for a critical procedure. That makes the whole ship hostage to a single individual who may get hurt or sick, leaving you in big trouble. In the current squeeze on business costs, many companies have cut back so much that they are only one-deep in critical positions, leaving no margin for error. I saw this as a prescription for disaster. My goal was to cross-train in every critical area. Thus, when the day came, I didn't let the experienced officer do it. I wanted other people to start learning.

I found myself on the bridge with a junior-grade lieutenant, K.C. Marshall—a great guy, always smiling—who was that watch's conning officer (the person who "conns" the ship orders the helmsman regarding its course and speed). I asked him if he had ever refueled at sea. He looked down at his feet and said, "No sir." He was afraid I would think him incompetent. Far from it. The problem was that he had never been given the opportunity to learn.

Next, I asked Lieutenant Jerry Olin, the officer of the deck, if he had ever run a refueling at sea. I got the same downward glance, the same "No sir." Olin actually thought I was going to relieve him.

I looked at both these fine young officers and said, "Guess what: I have never done it before either. It's time the three of us learned how." They both broke into ear-to-ear grins. (In truth, I had done it hundreds of times, though never on *Benfold*. I also had Kevin Hill on hand to coach and mentor the novices.)

While maneuvering alongside the tanker, Marshall was extremely tentative. The usual practice, I was told, was to wait to be directed in what to do. I don't need parrots in my organization. Marshall kept asking me for permission to change rudder by a degree or add half a knot to our speed.

If all you give are orders, then all you will get are order-takers.

Since my goal was to create self-starters, I finally said, "Hey, K.C., it's your ship, take responsibility for it. Don't ask permission; do it." That was all he needed to hear. I stood by in case of trouble, but I became irrelevant. He took complete control and did a fantastic job. I was truly proud of him, and his confidence soared. I burst with pride when I think of how far K.C. progressed as a naval officer.

The message raced through the ship: This captain doesn't want parrots—he wants people who think for themselves. That was my first opportunity to demonstrate a new style, and it paid off handsomely. Trusting a neophyte to perform this tricky maneuver was a powerful metaphor as well as the reality of my way of leading. Refueling at sea became a symbol for the positive changes that lay ahead.

But in all honesty, I have to say I was terrified at the start of the refueling. After all, I had never been fully responsible for this maneuver, and here I was, at thirty-six, in charge of a billion-dollar asset. I was filled with self-doubt, and my heart was racing. I was nearly hyperventilating; I wondered what kind of image I was projecting. I called my XO, Lieutenant Commander Jeff Harley, and asked him if I appeared nervous. He said he could not tell, and I had no choice but to believe him.

After we made our approach and settled in nicely alongside the tanker, I had a feeling of total relief; then I started to feel almost giddy at how well K.C. was doing. My own confidence started to soar, and I said to myself, "Hey, I can do this." Four days into my tenure, I started to feel that *Benfold* had the potential to be great and do great things. Looking back, that refueling was when I started to believe in myself as a leader.

TAKE A CHANCE ON A PROMISING SAILOR.

One of my first disciplinary cases on *Benfold* came just three weeks after I took command. A young sailor had stayed out late the night before we were to sail. He had forgotten to set his alarm, and we left without him. That's a serious offense, leaving a ship shorthanded in what might be a crisis—and it is obviously embarrassing to the captain.

At the time, the young man could have gone either way, could have become either a good sailor or a chronic misfit. In the end, I took a big chance on him. My trust was a calculated risk that I hoped would pay off.

First we had to handle the offense. We called him at his home in San Diego and told him to report to the commodore, who had him flown out to the ship on a helicopter. I wanted to show the crew that, unlike many other COs, I wasn't going to let such cases fester for months before acting. So the minute the copter touched down, we announced his arrival on the public-address system and told him to report for discipline. The rest of the crew noticed.

He was very up front and honest. He told me that he had stayed out too late, overslept, and was sorry. He took full responsibility for his actions. Personal accountability is a declining character trait in the United States today, so I took notice when he made no effort to shift the blame. I asked him how he thought I should penalize him. He recited the maximum penalty a captain can impose, fully expecting to be hit with it. I gave him about half of that, including thirty days' restriction to the ship, thirty days' extra duties, reduced rank, and half pay for two months.

I also made him write a letter of apology to his shipmates, acknowledging that he had let them down—that if the ship had needed him in an emergency or in combat, he would not have been there to be counted on. Recognizing that had a big impact on him. To this day, he still feels bad—not that he missed the ship's departure, but that he let down his shipmates. The letter appeared in the *Plan of the Day,* a daily newsletter that everyone reads.

The early signs were promising: He was doing all right. But while he was still on restriction, he made a special request to take a vacation so that he could fly home to see his mother. She was seriously ill, recovering from a major operation. The ship was scheduled for a six-month deployment, and if he didn't see his mother during the thirty days he was restricted, he would have to wait seven months.

Every level of his chain of command turned him down. Since he was serving time for a transgression, the request went against every aspect of Navy discipline. I agonized over it. If I were to approve it, I might be sending a signal to the crew that I was soft. The risk I was weighing, very consciously, was whether the crew would believe I was serious about what I said, or would shrug me off as full of empty words.

Finally, I approved his request. We gave him seven days of leave and tacked the week onto his restriction when he came back. He went home, visited his mother, and came back a new man. He was determined never to let me or his shipmates down again. He felt he had been treated fairly and was going to repay us by becoming the best sailor there was.

He trained himself to operate a very demanding watch station, monitoring the computer systems that handle secure transmission of enemy data between ships. This is one of the toughest positions for enlisted sailors in the combat information center. He became the best at it, not only on the ship, but in the whole battle group. I was so impressed by his performance that I reinstated him to his third-class petty officer rank.

When it was time for him to reenlist, he said he would if we would send him to air traffic controller school. That is an agonizing course; at least 50 percent flunk out of it. The entrance requirements include a clean disciplinary record and the minimum rank of second-class petty officer, and he was unqualified on both counts. But we went to bat for him and got an exemption. He graduated number one in his class and became the best air intercept controller I had seen.

The sailor ultimately left the Navy and is working for the defense contractor that makes the software he had become so expert at using. He is working to solve its design flaws. He and I still keep in touch by e-mail, and not long ago when I was in San Diego we met for breakfast with his father, who wanted to thank me for what I had done for his son. That was a nice breakfast, and I left with a good feeling. It is gratifying to know you have had a positive impact on people's lives, and then see them go on to greater things.

The Navy and the country will benefit immensely from his dedicated work for the defense contractor.

IF A RULE DOESN'T MAKE SENSE, BREAK IT.

In most Persian Gulf ports, alcohol isn't available, so most U.S. sailors don't exactly rush ashore. Dubai is different. It's one of the Gulf's few wet ports—an attractive city of about 300,000 people in the United Arab Emirates—and my first visit there started beautifully. Commanding officers get a car and driver, and I toured the town like a visiting pasha, stopping to have a Foster's Lager every now and then. In the meantime, five chartered buses were ferrying my crew to all the liberty spots, and it pleased me to imagine how much fun they were having.

I was wrong. When I met a sailor returning to our ship, I asked cheerily how he liked Dubai. He said he hated the place. So did his shipmates. This floored me. How could anyone hate Dubai?

The problem was the transportation. He explained that the buses were sixty-passenger rattletraps driven by demons who refused to stop when our sailors wanted to get off or on. Moreover, the Navy had ruled that sailors were restricted to using the buses to get around. Because of security concerns, they weren't even allowed to walk or take a taxi.

This was not the kind of experience my crew deserved, so I immediately got rid of the buses and hired twenty ten-passenger vans. That way, ten sailors could check out their own chauffeured van and go anywhere they wanted in Dubai and its environs.

However, hiring those vans violated Navy regulations. Many years ago, some well-meaning bean counter thought it would be cost-beneficial to require sixty-passenger buses for sailors on liberty. But I thought that cost had to be balanced with safety and the crew's experience. In my view, those behemoths were not only inconvenient, they were highly vulnerable targets. If one of them got hit by a terrorist, it might kill sixty sailors, whereas attacking one of my vans would cause ten casualties at worst.

This was not just a rationalization. My world had been rocked when terrorists blew up the Khobar Towers military complex in Saudi Arabia in the summer of 1996, killing nineteen airmen. I was with Secretary Perry at the time, and we flew to Riyadh to inspect the damage. We stood in the huge crater where the bomb had gone off. We saw the dormitory room where the force of the blast blew an airman into the ceiling and left an indented print of his body. We never discussed it, but it may have been William Perry's worst day as U.S. secretary of defense. I resolved then and there never to let that happen to anyone whose life had been entrusted to me.

Against regulations or not, the vans were the right thing to do. Overnight, my crew started enjoying Dubai, and I slept better knowing they were safer than before. I even assigned four people—two officers and two chief petty officers—to full-time duty as "fun coordinators," responsible for making sure that my sailors had the best possible shore liberties. For example, they spotted an advertisement in the *Khaleej Times,* the local newspaper, for an upcoming concert by the touring U.S. rapper Coolio. Fifty of our sailors went to the show, as well as fifty more from another ship, USS *O'Bannon*. Every day those minivans bopped around Dubai, taking my crew sand-skiing in the desert, swimming in mountain lakes, to a shopping mall, the theater, beach clubs, and restaurants. The town even had a Mexican eatery.

Who could dislike Dubai? The sailors from every other U.S. ship. They were still bouncing around in the big buses, hating every minute. Their displeasure eventually percolated up to Vice Admiral Tom Fargo, the three-star commanding the Fifth Fleet.

Like me, Fargo had assumed that Dubai was a great liberty town. It was an issue of class and rank. Commanding officers and admirals in their chauffered sedans loved Dubai; enlisted people could not wait to leave. Not long after we canned our rattletraps, Fargo was being driven through town with his executive assistant, ruefully wondering about the grumbling he had heard from sailors on other ships. His security-officer driver overheard him and asked permission to speak. The driver then gave the admiral an earful about the *Benfold* experience. Fargo was fascinated and immediately ordered his aide to have me churn out a written report of everything we had done.

Not knowing whether I would be reprimanded or cheered, I decided to fess up and wrote a five-page summary of how *Benfold* transformed Persian Gulf duty from onerous into a great trip. I described our improvised tools—music videos, light shows, and all the details of our Dubai caper, including the liberties I had taken with those illegal vans. Finally, I asked his help in getting the regulations changed.

Fargo came through. He sent my five-page manifesto to every ship in the Persian Gulf. I later heard that on the aircraft carrier *Nimitz*, the commanding officer met with all his senior people to decide how they could scale up our techniques for their sailors. Here I was, the most junior commanding officer in the Persian Gulf, and everyone was borrowing from our playbook. By the way, Tom Fargo is now a four-star admiral in charge of the entire Pacific Fleet. And it's okay for Navy ships to hire vans instead of buses.

IF A RULE DOES MAKE SENSE, BREAK IT CAREFULLY.

At the beginning of August of that year, two weeks before we were set to depart from San Diego, I told Master Chief Scheeler to load one hundred cases of beer on the ship and lock them up. He looked alarmed, as if he might be dealing with a closet loony.

In fact, he gave me the hundred-yard stare, totally dazed. Drinking alcohol is absolutely forbidden on Navy ships, and for good reason: Nautical lore bristles with stories of mutinies, shipwrecks, and other disasters fueled by alcohol.

"Captain," he said, "what are you going to do with a hundred cases of beer?"

"I haven't a clue," I answered, "but when the opportunity presents itself I don't want to be unprepared. And by the way, please get premium beer. I don't want my crew drinking anything substandard."

It was obvious from his expression that he wasn't exactly with the program. A week later, I asked where the beer was, and he said the chiefs hadn't ordered it yet. Why not?

"Well, sir, we just think it's a bad idea to load beer. We think the crew will get into trouble."

As a Pentagon alumnus, I know slow-rolling when I see it, and I was being slow-rolled. When people don't agree with you, they slow their actions till you are past the drop-dead date.

"Master Chief," I said calmly, "I want you to load a hundred cases of beer on my ship."

Three days later, he came back with the executive officer and both of them tried to change my mind. "You guys don't understand," I said. "I told you I want beer on this ship."

"There's no way we can talk you out of it?"

"No way whatsoever."

In short order, a huge eighteen-wheeler beer truck backed down the pier, and we proceeded to load eighty cases of Miller Genuine Draft and twenty cases of Rolling Rock. We put them under lock and key—and I had the key. No one could figure out when, if ever, we might actually drink the stuff. But you can't go into a combat zone without proper gear. That was the *Benfold* motto: Always be prepared.

By December 30, 1997, we had completed almost our entire one-hundred-day Gulf tour and still hadn't touched the beer. I was beginning to think the opportunity would never come.

The very next day, New Year's Eve, Saddam Hussein threw another fit. *Benfold* was ordered to leave Bahrain and get into position to fire our Tomahawk missiles at Iraq, if ordered. What upset everyone on board, including me, was that all the other ships were staying in Bahrain, where their crews could celebrate New Year's Eve at the Navy base. In effect, they were getting a prize for being less proficient with their cruise missiles than we were.

Fortunately, the crisis passed. And while we were standing by at sea on the afternoon of December 31, a heavy storm doused Bahrain with two inches of rain. Bahrain, alas, has no sewers. Two inches of not very clean water flooded the entire city. It knocked out the power plant and closed the Navy base. As a result, all sailors were restricted to their ships on New Year's Eve, with no alcohol.

Benfold was told to return to port if we wished. Instead, I set course for anchorage outside Bahrain and told my supply officer to chill the beer. He looked pained and perplexed. So did Master Chief Scheeler, who said, "Sir, I'd like to try and talk you out of serving beer on the ship."

"Master Chief," I answered, "I have no intention of serving beer on this ship."

"What are you cooling it down for?"

"We're going to have a cookout and drink beer, but not on the ship."

As we approached the anchorage, we were met by a huge

barge, probably fifty feet wide and three hundred feet long. I had arranged with our husbanding agent to have it towed there. We lowered our ladder to the barge and—presto!—we had, at least in my interpretation of regulations, access to a non-ship party space.

That night, while all the other sailors in the area spent a bone-dry New Year's Eve restricted to their ships, my people had a well-earned blast on our party barge, where the beer flowed, the cookout sizzled, the stereo boomed, and we all cheered the arrival of 1998. The one thing we didn't have was fireworks. (In hindsight, we could have rustled up a pretty decent pyrotechnic show with all the firepower we had on that ship.) Delighted to celebrate with friends in a way unique to *Benfold*—a way that honored their hard work—many sailors said it was the best New Year's Eve party they had ever attended. They were with not just shipmates, but comrades.

That's exactly how their captain felt, too.

CHAPTER EIGHT

GO BEYOND STANDARD PROCEDURE

⚓ IN THE NAVY, AS IN BUSINESS, SOP—STANDARD OPER-
ating procedure—tends to rule. After all, it's standard—safe, proven, effective. You will seldom get in trouble for
following standard operating procedure.

On the other hand, you will rarely get outstanding results. And
all too often, SOP is a sop—it distracts people from what's really
important. In my time in the Navy, we often let ourselves get deflected from our real priorities by petty bureaucratic inspections
or by the need to put on a good show for a visiting VIP. At times,

we seemed most concerned about getting the captain promoted to admiral. All these efforts detracted from our bottom-line goal—combat readiness.

Innovation and progress are achieved only by those who venture beyond standard operating procedure. You have to think imaginatively, but realistically, about what may lie ahead, and prepare to meet it. You have to look for new ways to handle old tasks and fresh approaches to new problems. As my friends at NASA would say, you have to push the envelope. And it's never easy.

KEEP YOUR PRIORITIES IN FOCUS.

I first learned this lesson in the Persian Gulf at 0430 on August 2, 1990, courtesy of Saddam Hussein. It was a moment of truth in my life, a defining event that has charted my course ever since.

At the time, I was a twenty-nine-year-old combat systems officer on USS *England,* an old cruiser equipped with long-range guided missiles to shoot down incoming aircraft. This was my fourth post since graduating from the Naval Academy in 1982, and I was still learning. The commanding officer of *England,* who was the aristocratic son of a diplomat, was difficult to work for; the XO was nearing retirement. I wasn't learning a great deal from either of them. Still, I did my best to master my complex job.

Peacetime naval deployment schedules get planned years in advance, so it had been decided back in 1988 that we would reach the Persian Gulf on August 2, 1990—which turned out to be the day Saddam invaded Kuwait. Ironically, the United States was drawing down its forces in the area at that time. We had no Army or Air Force personnel stationed in the region, and only five warships in the Gulf—four small frigates and the *England*—with no air cover.

At 0430, the general quarters alarm sounded on board. I leaped out of bed, rushed to my post still wiping the sleep from my eyes, looked at the radar screen, and saw twenty-one fighter jets coming right at us. The first thought that flashed through my mind was, "Holy shit." The second was, "My will is up to date and my life insurance is paid up."

Then the commanding officer asked me what I was going to do. I looked at him in total disbelief; I had been waiting for *him* to tell *me* what to do. I took a deep breath and told him that the fighters were about 120 miles away and our missiles had a maximum range of about 115 miles. I was going to open fire when the jets were at 80 miles. There was just one problem: We still didn't know whose jets they were. They were coming at us from the vicinity of Iraq, and since we didn't have any allies in that area, we could only assume they were hostile.

To call the ensuing minutes tense would be a great understatement. The jets kept getting closer and closer. At 82 miles—just as I was getting ready to launch the first missile salvo—they made a sudden right turn into Saudi Arabia. I'm sure my sigh of relief was heard down in the engine room. Hours later, Navy intelligence informed us that it had been the fleeing Kuwaiti air force. We came very close to a major fiasco because we didn't have the relevant information when we needed it.

The weeks that followed were anxious ones for us. There were very few U.S. or Allied forces in the Gulf, and we were vulnerable to attack from Saddam. Then help started arriving. An aircraft carrier came first, then jet fighters and Army units. We all know the final outcome: We won Operation Desert Storm because we used overwhelming force. But at the start, USS *England* was pretty much alone. Had Saddam come after us, the result would have been grim. Those early days were so tense that, after standing watch for six hours, I'd be too keyed up to sleep or even rest. During those long worrisome hours, I had a lot of time to think about how unprepared *England* truly was for battle.

The ship was not as combat-ready as it should have been; the officers could have done much more to make it so. Instead, we had spent too much time and effort putting on the obligatory tour for the visiting admiral. It was time that provided no value to the bottom line of combat readiness.

I made a solemn pledge to myself that if I ever had the opportunity to captain a ship, I would not flunk the challenge. I would focus on combat readiness, because without it people could die. I never wanted one of my sailors to go home in a body bag because I had failed as a leader. If we had taken casualties on that fateful day, I would have gone to my grave knowing that I hadn't done my best to prepare *England* for battle. Even as a junior officer, I could have insisted on training much harder and created better incentives for the crew to perform. It was a grave failure of leadership.

At 0430 that morning, as I watched those jets racing toward us, I had a wake-up call. I made a decision that from that day forward, any ship under my command would be battle-ready and manned by the most highly prepared, motivated, and respected sailors in the Navy. And there would be no distractions. We would constantly plan for "what if" situations: What if an enemy fighter was traveling in a commercial air route and suddenly veered toward us, threatening to attack? What if a terrorist boat tried to attack us in port? What if we had a major fire on the ship?

In battle, our initial reactions can often be the difference between success and failure, life and death. We also need to apply the successes and mistakes of others to our own situation and learn from them. If you prepare for the most challenging scenarios, chances are good that you will be much better prepared for the unforeseen.

STAY AHEAD OF THE COMPETITION.

A little forward planning can give you an enormous advantage.

For example, *Benfold* and two other ships—*Stethem* and *Lake Champlain*—were scheduled to perform an important exercise at sea. It called for us to line up in a column and prove our marksmanship by shooting down a simulated missile—a drone—with our own missiles. Launched from a plane, the drone presents a very small target. Each ship had to determine where the target was coming from, then fire two missiles to knock it out before it destroyed us. Our missiles travel at about 3,600 miles per hour.

These drones travel at about 500 miles per hour and are so expensive and carry such sophisticated test equipment that actually hitting one is rare. Sensors tell the drone controllers when a ship's missile is about to impact, so at the very last second, they maneuver it out of the way. The test equipment determines whether the ship would have scored a hit.

Typically, you just show up on the day of a missile shoot, perform the task, and sail away. But we wanted to excel, and in this case the feeling went deeper than usual. *Stethem* was a sister ship, a carbon copy of *Benfold* that was built at the same time in the same Mississippi shipyard, and both crews had a strong case of sibling rivalry. And *Lake Champlain,* an AEGIS cruiser, had become my archrival. I was a three-striper and the most junior commander in the Pacific Fleet. *Lake Champlain's* four-stripe captain was the most senior. It was natural, then, to want to outgun them in friendly competition. Time after time, *Benfold* outperformed *Lake Champlain.*

Actually, I didn't consider it rivalry; I didn't have any rivals. I was in competition only with myself, to have the best ship we possibly could. Inevitably, however, other commanders chafed when *Benfold* kept topping them, and whether I wanted it or not, rivalries emerged. To be honest, I enjoyed winning and I wasn't sensitive enough to avoid gloating, but I will return to discuss that further.

In this particular competition, we knew what winning would take. The drone knew precisely what our radar was picking up and could respond instantly. Realizing that the odds were against us in this challenge, and wanting to maximize a business opportunity, we started planning for the exercise three months in advance.

Lake Champlain's captain was in charge of the shootout, but he and his officers did little planning until the last minute. When they finally focused, it was too late for the crew to do a good job. By contrast, we were so organized that we gave ourselves a break and scheduled a port visit in San Francisco five days before the event.

Just as we pulled into San Francisco, I received an order from *Lake Champlain's* CO to turn around and rush south for a rehearsal off San Diego. I responded that we were on a port visit and were so well prepared for the shoot that we didn't need to rehearse. He reminded me that he was the senior commanding officer, and if I didn't attend the rehearsal he would ban us from the shoot, which would ruin *Benfold*'s readiness rating.

I took the liberty of forwarding that missive, without comment, to the three-star admiral's chief of staff in San Diego, Captain Ed Hebert. He promptly sent a message back to the CO of *Lake Champlain,* with copies to everyone else, saying that *Benfold* was free to do whatever it wished about the rehearsal. In the culture of the Navy, it was a pretty big deal to cast aside a senior officer's preferences in favor of a junior officer's.

I thought that *Lake Champlain*'s CO must have been a bit embarrassed, so I decided to do the right thing and show up for the rehearsal anyway. We cut short our San Francisco visit by twelve hours and raced *Benfold* south at thirty knots to take part in the practice.

We headed out of San Francisco into a spectacular sunset, with the crew manning the rails to enjoy it. In the bay's tricky currents, it might have been more prudent to leave by daylight, but again I was moving outside of standard procedure. My business was a 24/7 operation, and we needed to navigate proficiently at night. That sunset transit was a thoroughly memorable event.

The next day, a plane stood in for the drone and we practiced the communication procedures without actually shooting. *Benfold* was the first ship to detect the aircraft and the first to get out all the reports. Expecting my *Lake Champlain* colleague to resent losing the first round to *Benfold,* I figured that during the actual exercise he would order his crew to fire the first shot, which, I predicted, the drone was programmed to evade. In other words, shooting first would be a good way to miss the target and lose the award for competently defending your ship against incoming missiles.

"Don't be the first to shoot," I told my people. "Accuracy is more important. The only thing anyone will remember tomorrow is who hit the target, not who shot first. Just stay cool and make sure that both our shots are bull's-eyes."

As I predicted, *Lake Champlain* shot off a missile as soon as it detected the target, but the drone immediately evaded. *Stethem* shot both its missiles—both missed—before *Benfold* shot its first. *Lake Champlain* never got off its second missile. *Benfold* scored two direct hits. One ship's going to do better than the other. The point is to be sure to take responsibility as the CO, because how well the crew is prepared and how well it performs typically is a reflection of how well the CO leads.

PUSH THE ENVELOPE FOR INNOVATION.

On one of my trips out of the Pentagon with Secretary Perry, we visited a ship that had rigged a satellite TV system. Those sailors watched world news on CNN, and that ship was actually one of the best I had ever seen. When we boarded another ship without TV, the contrast was striking. The first crew knew about the events that might affect their lives, while the other ship was completely oblivious and could not have cared less. I realized, firsthand, the power of information. Those that have it prosper. Those that don't, wither.

Satellite TV was available only on carriers at the time, which meant just twelve of the Navy's three hundred ships. Perry told me to write a memo to the secretary of the Navy directing him to put satellite TV on these ships. I wrote the memo, but before sending it I decided to talk to a senior officer in the Navy's budget office to tip him off that this was coming and that they had better start budgeting for it. He said, "Mike, you can have the secretary of defense sign that memo. But there's no money in the budget for it, it isn't on our list of priorities, and it is never going to happen. I guarantee you we're going to wait you out on this one, and nothing is ever going to come of it."

I was dejected. Perry signed the memo, and I sent it to the secretary of the Navy, but I knew he had very little time left in office and nothing would happen. I stopped thinking about it; it was a lost cause.

Flash forward: *Benfold* had just arrived in the Persian Gulf. One of my officers came back from the Fifth Fleet's headquarters, where he had heard about a new program to fit out three ships to receive satellite TV at sea. Lo and behold, the Navy secretary had actually held the admirals' feet to the fire. I almost fell off my chair.

I had the officer in charge of our electronic equipment call the Pentagon and find out which three ships were destined to get this equipment. *Benfold* was not one of them. I called the Navy commander who was handling the program and explained who I was. When she found out I had written the memo, *Benfold* became number one on the list of ships to get the equipment.

The next day our satellite TV receivers were express-shipped to us in the Persian Gulf, and my crew spent the next two weeks figuring out how to install them. When they were done, *Benfold* was the only ship in the Gulf with satellite TV, except for the two carriers. We could get news, sports, even sitcoms. The crew felt honored. We used to tape-record football playoffs, and other ships would send over their helicopters to pick up a copy.

If we had stopped at standard operating procedure, had I not called the Navy commander in charge of the program, we would not have gotten the TV. But it was the right thing to do to fight for it, just as it was right for Perry to push for it in the first place. That equipment is now being installed on every ship in the Navy, and it is doing wonders for the morale, not to mention performance, of ships on long sea duty.

VOLUNTEERING BENEFITS EVERYONE.

In my interviews with the crew, I got feedback in ways I never imagined. After we implemented the lower deck's ideas on how to improve the way we did business, the ship's energy began heating up. Performance leaped, along with morale and reenlistments. I was beginning to feel very good about myself as a leader.

My hubris was promptly punctured. One day I asked a nineteen-year-old sailor how he liked *Benfold*. He said he hated the ship and was getting out of the Navy as soon as possible. That crushed me; how could anyone hate my ship? But I recovered. I told him he was a great electronics technician, and when he got out of the Navy I would help him get a job in the electronics industry. He said he hated electronics and would have nothing to do with it in civilian life. I asked what he did want to do, and he said he wanted to be a social worker.

In my ignorance, I actually chuckled and informed him that social workers don't make any money. I said I could get him a job paying $60,000 to $80,000 a year. All he had to do was stick with electronics, the wave of the future. I must have sounded like the pompous businessman in the movie classic *The Graduate* who gives young Dustin Hoffman the secret password to fame and fortune—"Plastics."

I will never forget that teenage sailor's response. He said he had spent his whole life in and out of foster homes; he wanted to help make sure that what happened to him did not happen to other children. I felt as small as a man could. I had just had my core values calibrated by someone half my age.

I was really shaken by this experience, and spent about a week sitting in my bridge wing chair staring at the sea. The obvious answer finally hit me: I should use my future social worker's talents right now. I called him to come up, and told him that his next mission was to find a local elementary school in San Diego that we could adopt.

When we pulled back into port, he spent a week searching for the right school. When he found it, I told him to round up as many shipmates as he could and find out what the school needed. He gathered forty of his shipmates, kids on the lowest rung of the economic ladder, and established a relationship with the school, painting the building for openers. They went on to mentor elementary school students after school, read to them, and help them with math.

I never took attendance. I didn't know who was going except for the original social worker. But whenever we were back from sea duty, sailors could always be found at the school tutoring, coaching, and doing anything else they were asked to. And the idea of community service spread: Whenever we pulled into a foreign port, forty or fifty sailors would go off and find an orphanage or hospital that could use a few helping hands.

Benfold made us all proud in so many ways that it is hard to single out one achievement above the others. But for me, the one that stands out was the volunteer spirit we created throughout the ship. It was heartwarming to see these young people, almost all of them from underprivileged backgrounds, giving of themselves to make things better for others, and not because they had to, but because they wanted to.

I know that government programs do a lot of good and help a lot of people, but only local communities really understand the nuances of their challenges. One-size-fits-all programs tend to fit none. I think business has to pick up some of the slack. It is good for morale, good for your reputation, and good for your soul. Companies are right there in the community, and they can target their efforts to where they're most needed. It really isn't complicated. The need is there, staring them in the face, and filling it benefits everyone—those who do as well as those who receive.

I recently spoke to a group of managers at a nuclear power plant, which are often the subject of controversy and have to be recertified periodically, a process that includes public hearings. One of the considerations is the plant's track record as a member of the community.

Before I was to speak I talked to my mother, who is eighty and, after teaching English and typing for forty-one years, is still called in as a substitute. The school district in Altoona, Pennsylvania, pays substitute teachers $55 a day. You do the math. Look at the value we are placing on education. Mom told me that she was teaching calculus, math, geometry, and chemistry—subjects in which she has no expertise. I learned later that other school districts were hiring high school graduates to be substitute teachers. What's wrong with this picture?

Now most of the people who run nuclear power plants have advanced degrees in physics and math and other tough subjects. It struck me that the plant should partner with the local school district, so that when they need a substitute teacher, a plant employee could take a day off and pitch in. A company could easily set up a program to give people a day or two a year to volunteer as substitutes. It would be a win/win situation for everyone: good for the school district and good for the company, and it would do wonders for the employees to get away from the routine of work, go back to school, and make a difference in children's lives. I can't think of a downside for anyone involved.

The head of the power plant told me he was going to pursue the idea. I hope every manager who reads this will follow his lead.

GO FOR THE OBVIOUS.
IT'S PROBABLY A WINNER.

Sometimes a solution is so simple and so apparent that we ignore it. We think it isn't innovative or cool or complex enough, or that others have considered and discarded it. That's a big mistake.

While *Benfold, Gary,* and *Harry W. Hill* were in the South China Sea en route to Singapore, we got word that a German naval task force was heading toward us on the way to Japan. The German navy rarely strays from NATO waters, but this squadron was touring the western Pacific. We were told to plan an encounter with the German navy and see what kind of training we could work out. The task fell to the senior commanding officer on USS *Gary,* and I saw it as a huge opportunity. I was excited about it and came up with a plan to simulate the German ships as the enemy and conduct a battle at sea. Then we would exchange personnel to visit one another's ships, and we would do joint maneuvers in the South China Sea.

The two other captains didn't care much about this. But I argued that we were at sea, there was nothing else to do, and we might as well have fun and get some training out of it. It turned out to be a great learning experience. We transferred people from ship to ship. We refueled from the Germans' oiler. We sent them over several cases of Miller Genuine Draft and Rolling Rock. We learned a lot about working with our allies, and they learned a lot about us. It was a wonderful opportunity.

Sometimes people are myopic. They get into a set pattern, and they can't envision the potential benefits they could glean from various situations. Our great training exercise with the German navy in the South China Sea almost didn't happen because some didn't think it was important.

DON'T WORK HARDER. WORK SMARTER.

Not long after we returned to San Diego in early 1998, *Benfold* entered a commercial shipyard for nine weeks of maintenance, during which the equipment was dismantled and rebuilt to extend its life. All well and good—except that the process was a mess.

A beautiful ship is torn apart and soon gets covered with dirt, oil, and grime. To most of the shipyard employees, it's just another construction site, loaded with cables, pipes, and steel plates. Making sure they don't break anything is a full-time monitoring task, and no fun whatsoever. You're always dirty. You always wear a hard hat and earplugs because of the danger and noise, and the work is badly coordinated. One day a painting crew will leave passageways fresh and sparkling. Next day, riggers will haul equipment through, leaving scratches in their wake, or electricians will rip up freshly sanded decks to get at wires underneath.

You would think that shipyards would be full of smart project managers skilled at coordinating these jobs, but in my experience no one ever thought of automating the process. I spoke to my lieutenant, Jerry Olin, who had now become one of my "go-to ninjas."

"We can do this better," I said. "We can help the shipyard. We can show them how to dovetail all these jobs so that nothing ever has to be redone, and the whole project gets finished on schedule, if not sooner."

It wasn't easy, but with the help of Petty Officer Derrick Thomas and his experience with databases, Jerry created a computer tracking system to manage the nine-week overhaul process. We also sent half our crew to school for training that they could not get on the ship, so we were doing this with a vastly reduced workforce. We were trying to juggle a million balls in the air, and Jerry never dropped one. All in all, we were maximizing the return on taxpayer dollars.

It soon became clear that we would finish the work in seven weeks instead of nine, a feat that was unheard of. I immediately requested permission to move *Benfold* back to our pier at the naval station, where it was cleaner. The answer—you guessed it— was no. The logic, and I use the word loosely, was classic bureaucracy-think: We contracted to keep you there for nine weeks; you stay there nine weeks. But that's stupid, I said. Response: We pay this shipyard $10,000 a day in rent even if you're not there. It's in the contract. Do you really want us to throw away $10,000 a day?

I tried to argue that it made more sense to spend the $140,000 and get *Benfold* back to its berth and operational readiness, rather than let the ship and its crew go to pot for two weeks. I had a miserable fight over this and used up a lot of political capital in the process. But finally my betters retreated, and we left the shipyard two weeks ahead of schedule.

Then the budget figures arrived. Our budget for the nine weeks was $3 million, and we brought it in at about $2.2 million. Not only had we gotten the work done right the first time two weeks ahead of schedule, we had also cut the cost by some 25 percent, far more than we had "wasted" by leaving the yard early. When was the last time a Department of Defense project was finished flawlessly, under budget, and ahead of schedule? What's more, unlike other ships, we left the yard with *Benfold* absolutely spotless—our computerized system had factored in cleanup and repainting.

The president of the yard was dumbfounded. He just could not restrain himself from claiming that it was all due to his caring, meticulous civilian workers. That was nonsense, to say the least, but I wasn't going to argue the point. My boss knew how it happened. We didn't work any harder than anyone else; we worked smarter.

I applied the same principle to attack an epidemic of mechanical failures that was sweeping all the Arleigh Burke class destroyers in the Atlantic and Pacific Fleets.

These ships, including *Benfold,* have an enormous demand for electricity, which they get from gas turbine generators. The ship can run on two of them, with a third on board for emergencies.

The generators operate like jet engines, at enormous speed. Their critical cooling mechanism is a heat exchanger that runs seawater through metal tubes in the lubricating oil reservoir. The generators cost upward of $1.5 million each, but some designer had decided to save money by using cheap metal for the reservoir tubes. The tubes cost about $7,000. The upshot was that the tubes corroded, the pipes cracked, seawater contaminated the oil, and the motors broke down.

When *Benfold* lost two generators in a very short period of time and had to limp back to port, I started digging and found out that there had been around sixty similar failures. I wrote a message to the three-star admiral in San Diego blasting the design. It was then that he realized not only had this cost the Navy $60 million in lost generators, but that we could not replace them fast enough, so the Navy was losing combat capability.

An obvious solution was to replace the tubes with a tougher alloy, such as Monel. But something more might be needed, and the way the Navy worked, I knew it would take a year of studies before anything was approved. I needed a fix now, because I was down to one generator.

We took one of our broken lube oil coolers to a local engineering shop, where we had Monel tubes installed. We tested it and it worked, so we fixed the other one, and those heat exchangers are working to this day.

As I tell my people, when you see a bad trend developing, you need to yell and holler until people pay attention to it. My flagging the breakdowns let the admiral push the Navy to focus on the broader problem, but meanwhile, I was able to make my own fix by taking another kind of initiative. The point is, none of it happened by simply following standard procedure.

DON'T FIGHT STUPIDITY. USE IT.

The Navy's rules insisted on restricting young sailors to their ships when they arrived in overseas ports. The admirals were sure that these lusty young people would get into trouble as soon as they stepped on dry land in a foreign country—to say nothing of what could happen if they were to have a beer. We went to great places—Australia, Japan, Singapore, Thailand—which of course the sailors wanted to see. After all, the recruiting posters had promised they would see the world. But according to the Navy, they weren't mature enough to resist whatever temptations might present themselves.

The Navy expected these people to risk their lives in combat, but it was treating them as infants. I would be the last to claim that sailors on liberty always act in ways that make the Navy proud, but this rule was both stupid and insulting. The last straw came when a clever admiral in headquarters devised an insidious plan to minimize shore leave.

His idea was linked to the Navy's Enlisted Surface Warfare Specialist (ESWS) program, a superb system designed to train sailors beyond their specialties so they can learn how their entire ship works. With this training, they can backstop others. Everyone's skills are enhanced and the ship's performance as a whole is strengthened, particularly in a crisis.

When USS *Cole* was bombed in Yemen in 2000, it might very well have sunk if all hands knew only their own areas of duty. Instead, enough people understood the overall rescue plan and how their areas of expertise affected it. This additional knowledge was critical in their efforts to save the ship. This is the equivalent of a salesperson understanding the workings of finance, marketing, product development, human resources—the entire structure of the company. Sailors who complete ESWS wear a special pin on their uniforms and earn bonus points toward promotion. It is so difficult that only the most experienced sailors usually try to qualify.

The admiral, intent on limiting shore leave, decided that no one under twenty-one could stay ashore in a foreign port after midnight unless he or she had qualified for ESWS. It might have been a noble policy if the idea had been to encourage people to get qualified. Instead, the wording of the directive left the clear impression that it was intended to deprive people of a right rather than enhance a process.

Now, if I had blatantly disregarded the admiral's directive, I could have been fired. More important, my actions would have sent a message to my crew that it was all right to ignore policies you don't agree with.

But if I could not change a stupid rule, I could use it for my own purposes. I could try to interest the crew in qualifying for the program, which would get them liberty and, more to the point, increase the readiness of our ship. However, since hardly anyone had passed ESWS in my predecessor's time, the crew was convinced that it was unattainable so few even attempted it. In fact, *Benfold*'s ESWS program was so hard that I'm not sure I could have passed it myself.

My goal was to change that perception. Because I was proud of *Benfold*, I often invited guests to join me in touring the ship, and it occurred to me that, in a sense, the ESWS program basically taught sailors to be tour guides. In this context, a good tour guide would explain how the engines, generators, and weapons systems work; how we control aircraft; the mechanics of the anchors; and much more. ESWS qualifiers understood and could describe how the ship's many parts interact to make it a fighting machine.

I reviewed and streamlined the qualification process, removing about fifteen percent of the requirements because they weren't relevant to *Benfold*. Then I gathered all the sailors together and explained that ESWS was a good way for them to learn how to show guests around the ship. Once we defined it in those terms, the sailors became confident: "Hey, we can do this. Plus, it will help us get promoted." And somehow, word got out that an ESWS pin would also entitle underage sailors to liberty.

Nearly every sailor aboard joined the program. By the time we pulled into Bahrain on October 3, I was able to qualify my first junior sailor as an Enlisted Surface Warfare Specialist. He was Fireman Joseph Cotton, twenty years old and deservedly proud of his achievement.

We soon got word that General Anthony Zinni, the four-star Marine who was commanding the entire Middle East force, wanted to tour our ship. Hmmm, I thought, what a fortunate co-incidence.

I assembled all my junior enlisted people on the flight deck for the general's arrival. Among them was Fireman Cotton, my designated star for the occasion. General Zinni came aboard with Vice Admiral Tom Fargo, the U.S. ambassador to Bahrain, their security details, and a passel of aides. I asked the general if he would do Fireman Cotton the honor of pinning an ESWS pin on him. He was happy to oblige. For generals and admirals, pinning awards on sailors is the equivalent of politicians kissing babies.

"And now, sir," I said, "the ship is ready for your inspection."

"Lead the way," the general said.

"Another time, sir. Today, Fireman Cotton will give you the tour."

"Say again?"

"Fireman Cotton will escort you."

The general stood staring, trying to figure me out. His four stars glinted in the sun. He and Cotton were at polar ends of the military pay scale.

"Sir," I said, "the tour is part of the requirements for earning that pin, and I have the utmost confidence in Fireman Cotton. He knows the ship as well as I do."

Zinni was stunned that I would give up my face-time and let an enlisted man escort a four-star. That this poised twenty-year-old neither choked nor forgot his lines, and that his knowledge of the ship was quite sophisticated, shocked the general, but pleased him enormously. It was a grand slam.

That evening General Zinni was scheduled to speak about leadership at the Navy's birthday ball. As he was driving to the ball, Tom Fargo later told me, he ripped up his speech and made notes for another. The new talk focused on leadership on USS *Benfold,* specifically how we empowered our young sailors to assume major responsibilities—including giving calm, expert tours of the ship to VIPs so high on the food chain that officers on other ships would probably stutter in their presence. Zinni's listeners got the message. That was *Benfold*'s day to shine—the day we started earning our reputation as the go-to ship in the Persian Gulf.

After the Cotton-Zinni tour, the crew saw how serious I was about the ESWS program and their zeal redoubled. We soon qualified almost 200 of our 310 sailors, all of whom took great pride in wearing the pin. In turn, I could be proud of sailors who understood how the entire ship operated, exponentially increasing our combat readiness.

There is no downside to having employees who know how every division of an organization functions. The challenge is finding incentives to motivate them to want to do so. In our case, it was easy; 200 sailors were not only proud to wear their ESWS pins, they got liberty they otherwise would be denied.

CHAPTER NINE

BUILD UP YOUR PEOPLE

LEADERSHIP, AS I HAVE SAID, IS MOSTLY THE ART OF doing simple things very well. However, we sometimes make it far tougher than it needs to be. Unlike some leaders, I prefer to build myself up by strengthening others and helping them feel good about their jobs and themselves. When that happens, their work improves, and my own morale leaps.

I left drill-sergeant bullying to other leaders with other goals. Running *Benfold* demanded brains and initiative, not brawn. Only competent and self-confident sailors could handle the ship's complexities and fulfill its missions. These sailors could not be sculpted into a fighting crew by ruling with fear and punishing them as though they were inept kids. My job was to turn kids into grown-ups who would make Edward Benfold proud.

I focused on building self-esteem. I know that most of us carry around an invisible backpack full of childhood insecurities, and that many sailors often struggled under the load of past insults, including being scorned at home or squashed at school. I could make the load either heavier or lighter, and the right choice was obvious. Instead of tearing people down to make them into robots, I tried to show them that I trusted and believed in them.

Show me a manager who ignores the power of praise, and I will show you a lousy manager. Praise is infinitely more productive than punishment—could anything be clearer? But how many managers give this fact more than lip service? How many really live it? Not enough.

The same principle applies when you're dealing with bosses: Never tear them down; help them grow strong. If you want to achieve anything in a large bureaucracy, get inside the bosses' heads. Anticipate what they want before they know they want it. Take on their problems; make them look so good that you become indispensable. When they can't get along without you, they will support nearly anything you seek to accomplish.

LITTLE THINGS MAKE BIG SUCCESSES.

Within a couple of months of my taking over, other ship commanders began visiting *Benfold* to find out how we were getting our sailors to work so well. I was delighted to share all our secrets. They were hardly profound; mainly, we were attentive to people's feelings and potential. A lot of seemingly small gestures added up to a friendly and supportive atmosphere.

For example, I ordered a big supply of greeting cards that read, "The Officers and Crew of the USS *Benfold* Wish You a Happy Birthday." Each month my ship's office gave me a birthday list of my sailors' spouses. I would write, say, "Dear Marie" at the top and sign it "Love, Mike." Every card included my P.S. saying, "Your husband or wife is doing a great job," even if he or she were not. I knew the cards worked because sailors often came by to express their appreciation. It was my way of bringing their families into our orbit.

The CO of one of our sister ships loved the idea and immediately ordered his executive officer to send out birthday cards to the spouses of all his sailors. Of course he meant they should be sent out at the appropriate time—on the spouses' birthdays. The next day a year's worth of cards went out on the same day in one huge batch. Ouch. But in fact, this was symptomatic of that ship—the officers were good, but they sometimes didn't get things quite right. They weren't *Benfold*'s officers. I think they hit a performance ceiling because they didn't create a supportive climate that encouraged sailors to reach beyond their own expectations. Ultimately, that was *Benfold*'s edge.

I observed that most of my young sailors came from hardscrabble backgrounds and had struggled to make it into the Navy. I put myself in their parents' shoes and imagined how they would feel if they got letters from their kids' commanding officer, and I imagined how the kids would feel when their parents told them. I began writing letters to the parents, especially when their sons or daughters did something I could honestly praise. When the letters arrived, the parents invariably called their children to say how proud they were of them. To this day, I get Christmas cards from grateful parents.

One young man who wasn't star material was working on a project with four outstanding sailors. I debated whether he deserved one of my letters; because he was part of a stellar group, I went ahead. His parents were divorced, so I sent a letter to each parent. About two weeks later, the sailor knocked on my door with tears streaming down his face.

"What's wrong?" I asked.

"I just got a call from my father, who all my life told me I'm a failure. This time, he said he'd just read your letter, and he wanted to congratulate me and say how proud he was of me. It's the first time in my entire life he's actually encouraged me. Captain, I can't thank you enough."

My own tear ducts held, but I was very moved.

One of my true star sailors was a second-class petty officer, Darren Barton, of Little Rock, Arkansas. Darren was one of the sailors who did an outstanding job with the Tomahawk cruise missiles. I wrote his mother, Carol, about how well her son had performed, and she was so proud that one day, when President Clinton was visiting Little Rock, she staked out his motorcade and asked him to countersign my letter. She sent me a copy of that letter signed by the president of the United States, and I was extremely happy to share in her pride of her son.

My officers knew that they could always use me in their leadership toolkits. They never hesitated to knock on my door and say, "Hey, Captain, next time you're out walking around the ship, Sonarman Smith really aced that databank," or "Seaman Jones is doing a helluva job in the laundry. Could you stop by and tell him how much you appreciate him?"

Those conversations were the highlight of my day, and they didn't cost me or the Navy a dime. The more I went around meeting sailors, the more they talked to me openly and intelligently. The more I thanked them for hard work, the harder they worked. The payoff in morale was palpable. I'm absolutely convinced that positive, personal reinforcement is the essence of effective leadership. Yet some leaders seem to be moving away from it. They stay connected electronically with e-mail and cell phones, but they're disconnected personally, and many leaders almost never leave their offices. People seem to think that if you send somebody a compliment online, it's as good as the human touch. It is not. It's easier, but much less effective. Social interaction is getting lost in a digital world that trades more in abstractions than in face-to-face relations. It's more than a shame—it's a bottom-line mistake.

As I have said before, my sister Connie works for a major bank. One of her people did a phenomenal job, making hundreds of thousands of dollars for the bank, and Connie's boss sent an e-mail congratulating and thanking her. That very afternoon, he rode the elevator with her and didn't even acknowledge her existence. It completely wiped out any good his e-mail could have done.

Recall how you feel when your own boss tells you, "Good job." Do your people (and yourself) a favor. Say it in person, if you can. Press the flesh. Open yourself. Coldness congeals. Warmth heals. Little things make big successes.

The Navy has a program that assigns an ombudsman for every ship as a contact point for sailors' families. The idea is to make it as easy as possible to keep families informed of new orders, events aboard ship, the ship's movements, in general, and, of course, to have a communications link between sailors and their families. In practice, the ombudsman is usually the spouse of someone on the ship and is the hub for all the other families wanting to keep in touch with their relatives on board. We set out to make *Benfold*'s ombudsman program the best in the Navy, and in fact our ombudsman was phenomenal.

Sylvia Schanche had a special phone line for families to call and leave messages for her, which she responded to by calling the ship or sending an e-mail. She kept everyone informed about the ship's changing schedule; if there was an accident on board, we told her immediately what was happening and she passed the word to the families of anyone involved. If there was a death in a sailor's family, the ombudsman would make the arrangements to fly him or her back to the States. If a relative was hospitalized, she passed information back and forth. She even helped families who were having trouble coping with the stress of separation. She was a great resource and another way of keeping the crew strong and united. The less they have to worry about home, the more time and attention they have for the ship.

Most businesses should have a similar program, but hardly any do. For instance, I know of a manager who had a heart attack while on the road, but the company had no procedure in place to fly his family out to be with him in the hospital, and in general to ease a time of trauma. Personnel departments aren't usually organized to do that.

In fact, many of the techniques that I developed in the Navy could be easily adapted for personal reinforcement in the civilian workplace. For example, the Navy hands out medals for superior performance, but not when a sailor leaves the service. Leaving is perceived as breaking ranks and mildly inconsiderate of those left behind. I disagreed with that policy, believing that medals send two important signals even when they are given to departing people. They tell those leaving that their services have been valued; equally important, they show those remaining that their hard work will be recognized in the same way when they leave.

The commanding officer of a ship is authorized to hand out 15 medals a year. I wanted to err on the side of excess, so in my first year I passed out 115. Nearly every time a sailor left, I gave him or her a medal. Even if they hadn't been star players, they got medals in a public ceremony as long as they had done their best every day. I delivered a short speech describing how much we cherished the recipient's friendship, camaraderie, and hard work. It wasn't unusual for people to cry at those ceremonies. Sometimes the departing sailor's shipmates told funny stories, recalling his or her foibles, trials, and triumphs.

The award I handed out was called the Navy Achievement Medal. I often think that every company should have an equivalent—the General Electric Quality Star, say, or the IBM Order of Excellence, or the Microsoft Medal of Distinction. There is absolutely no downside to this symbolic gesture, provided it is done sincerely and without hype.

TRUST PEOPLE. THEY USUALLY PROVE YOU'RE RIGHT.

Once a year, all Navy ships undergo a thorough assessment, in which outside inspectors validate the ship's readiness. The ship as a whole and the crew's abilities and proficiencies are rated in twenty-four categories, on a scale ranging from basic Level One to advanced Level Four.

The purpose is to determine how much additional training the crew needs to be ready for combat. But if you assume that the higher a ship's level, the less time it would spend training at sea, you would be wrong. In fact, regardless of its readiness rating, every ship spends the next six months training at sea.

Thus there was no incentive to reach Level Four, and in fact, no ship ever did. Level One was the required minimum, and that was usually considered good enough.

Then *Benfold* came along.

Originally, my goal was to reach an overall rating of Level Two, but when I recognized the enormous potential of my crew, I raised the bar to Level Three, much to the chagrin of those who saw it as a quantum leap in their labor and my hubris.

I must also admit that, in addition to my noble motive of making the ship as good as it could be, I wanted to blow my archrival out of the water. Their assessment was scheduled to begin the week following ours. My rival's strategy was to do little and attain basic Level One. The CO had no idea that we were laying the groundwork to shake things up a little. In fact, we were about to rock his world.

Our first challenge was finding enough senior people to supervise the twenty-four areas of testing. My combat systems officer hit me with the unexpected news that we had only twenty qualified people who were not involved in other critical operations.

Thinking fast, I said, "Fine—pick supervisors from the next group down. You don't always need a senior person in charge. It could be a young, third-class petty officer."

"That's never been done before," he said.

"See what they can do," I said. "The alternative is to do nothing, right? Let's assign senior people to the most demanding areas and work our way down to the junior ones. If we don't get Level Three in some categories, so what? We will get Level One or Two. We have nothing to lose."

As it turned out, the third- and second-class petty officers were so honored to be chosen that they worked hard enough for several of their teams to outshine those supervised by senior people. The search-and-seizure team was particularly impressive. We assigned it to one of the ship's most junior sailors because we suspected he had the ability to honcho it. The outside inspectors protested, saying they could not validate the work of an important team that wasn't headed by a commissioned officer. But I insisted, and the young sailor did such a fantastic job that the inspectors ate their words and placed us at Level Four in that category.

Breaking out of our stratified systems to trust the people who work for us, especially those at or near the low end of the hierarchy, was a useful, progressive change. It let us unleash people with talent and let them rise to levels that no one had expected, simply by challenging them: Make *Benfold* the readiest ship afloat. In that context, how could we not have done well?

The huzzahs for our incredible performance were just rolling in as another ship was starting the assessment process. Its skipper, sensing disaster, exhorted his people to forget about Level One and shoot for Level Four.

But you can't "order" an outstanding performance. You have to plan, enable, nurture, and focus on it. Indeed, that ship finished at Level One.

Four months later the Navy's top boss, the chief of naval operations, streamlined the assessment process and settled on a formal program that allowed ships to skip the six-month training process if they could achieve the same performance levels that the *Benfold* had managed. This model is now standard throughout the Navy. And it came about because we delegated responsibility to people who were ready and able to accept it.

NEWBIES ARE IMPORTANT. TREAT THEM WELL.

One of the things the Navy was absolutely miserable at, as are many companies, was welcoming new employees. Recruits were sent to the Navy boot camp at Great Lakes, Illinois, just outside Chicago. They graduated on a Friday morning, boarded a plane in the afternoon, and landed in San Diego that night. And somehow they found their way to the ship—to be greeted by no one. Worse still, no one even knew they were coming. After enduring boot camp, their first encounter with the actual Navy was to walk in on a bunch of sailors who were getting ready for weekend leave and would have no time for them.

I started talking with new arrivals, asking them about their first day. They said they felt totally intimidated, that they had no friends and knew no one. They were lost for the first forty-eight hours, on their own aboard ship while nearly everyone else was on leave. I was seventeen when I first entered the Naval Academy, and I remember how scared I was. If that was frightening for me, I could imagine what arriving in San Diego must have been like for these young men and women.

I called my XO, Lieutenant Commander Harley, into my cabin. "What's our welcome-aboard program?" I asked.

"I don't have a clue," he answered.

"Well, go find out and report back to me."

The next day he was back in my cabin.

"Captain, the news is pretty embarrassing. We do nothing to prepare for their arrival."

"You have a five-year-old daughter," I told him. "Twelve years from now she may join the Navy. How would you want her treated on that first day?"

"I'd want her treated very well," he said.

Every sailor who reports to us is someone's son or daughter. We owe it to them to treat their kids well. It is our duty.

"What's the first thing you'd want her to do if she was seventeen and just showing up on ship?"

"I'd want her to call home and tell me she'd arrived safely."

"Bingo! Why not bring them up to my cabin and they can call their parents or boyfriends or girlfriends and tell them that they have arrived and are okay? With the government's telephone rates, a thirty-minute call will cost Uncle Sam only ninety cents. It will be the best ninety cents the Department of Defense ever spent."

We designed our welcome-aboard program. We found out who we were getting from boot camp, what flights they would be on, and we met them at the airport to bring them to the ship. Since I didn't sleep on the ship when it was in port, the command duty officer met the new people on the quarterdeck, shook their hands, brought them to my cabin, and let them call home. Their beds were made, their names were on their lockers, and the best performers from their divisions, assigned to be their "Running Mates," led them on a tour of the ship.

The next morning the Running Mates drove them all over the

base, pointing out the gym, the pool, the theater, the commissary, the medical and dental facilities. They also got the hot skinny on base life—inside info that's very important to a seventeen-year-old just stepping out into the world: who and what to avoid, and why; or warnings about, say, places not to go after dark, because they could be attacked or robbed. The Running Mates acted as tour guides, showing them San Diego's Sea World and the Hotel del Coronado. We wanted these young men and women to feel as though San Diego were their new home and we were their new family.

For their first five workdays on the ship, they weren't allowed to stray from their Running Mates. And within the first forty-eight working hours, they came to see me for a get-to-know-each-other talk. I greeted each the same way: "Welcome . . . I appreciate having you on our ship."

In addition to welcoming these new hires, the program was designed to infect the jaded vets with their enthusiasm. All too often, a gung-ho newcomer runs smack into a poisoned corporate culture that sucks the enthusiasm right out of her. I wanted the newcomers to remain so revved up that they would recharge the batteries of those who no longer felt that way.

Think about the welcome-aboard program in your company. Do newcomers arrive for the first day of work and find that no computer awaits them, their pay and benefits are delayed by red tape, and the only employee available to answer their questions is second-rate because the best people are too busy? If so, it isn't surprising that they become discontented with their jobs and disparage the organization. It's the end of their idealism.

I wanted *Benfold*'s environment to be exactly the opposite, and it was. Our new sailors appreciated our efforts, which paid tremendous dividends in the form of workforce enthusiasm and self-confidence. Once people heard about it, our Running Mate program was adopted by many other ships on the San Diego waterfront. The commander of our destroyer squadron even made a home movie about the welcome-aboard process for other ships.

BE THE RISING TIDE THAT LIFTS ALL BOATS.

Since World War II, and possibly before, the Navy has issued foul-weather jackets that are made of ugly blue duckcloth that keeps you neither dry nor warm. To my young sailors, they were a fashion statement not worth making. While browsing in a marine gear store, one sailor spotted a civilian version he loved—it was made of flashy blue Gore-Tex with reflective stripes and a built-in flotation device. Naturally, he told me about it immediately. The Navy jackets cost $150 apiece; these were $90 and superior in every way. They would actually keep you warm and dry, and they'd be safer than the standard issue because of the flotation device. And, as a bonus, *"USS Benfold"* could be stenciled on the back. Not your usual U.S. Department of Defense procurement, this was more value for less money.

"Great idea, sign me up," I said. We used the ship's credit card to buy 310 jackets and passed them out to all hands. We had a very cool-looking crew.

The next day, when another ship pulled into our pier, its sailors saw our sailors wearing the jackets. Half an hour later, that ship's command master chief strode over to say, "My captain has ordered you to stop wearing those jackets."

"Really? Why?" I asked.

"We almost had a mutiny over there—our crew wants the same jackets."

Had that ship's captain not been one of the most senior commanding officers in the Pacific Fleet, I would have laughed in the master chief's face. According to Navy protocol, the senior officer present is responsible for a pier's security, and he had decided that pier security was endangered because his sailors coveted my sailors' jackets.

"Why not just buy the same jackets for your people?" I asked.

"They'd steal them," he said. "Before we pull into port, we collect all our foul-weather jackets and lock them up. Can't trust these people."

What a difference between ships: We never worried about *Benfold* sailors stealing their jackets. They could wear them home if they wanted to. In fact, they were so proud of the new ones that they rarely took them off.

I told this gentleman that I considered his captain's order illegal and I refused to obey it. If he insisted, I said, I would be happy to go to the admiral's office and accept an immediate court-martial.

If that was an overreaction, I considered it justified. In part, I was remembering an incident that occurred while I was working for Defense Secretary Perry.

The four military services use their personnel budgets in very different ways. The Air Force stresses quality of life: Its people get beautiful housing, great bases, and excellent medical care. The Army and Marine Corps take nearly the opposite attitude. A very comfortable Air Force base could be next door to an Army base where soldiers are living in slums. But this was becoming embarrassing, so while I was in the Pentagon, the Army and Marine

Corps asked Perry to take money out of the Air Force budget and give it to them so they could upgrade their bases. He pondered their request for a few moments, then refused, telling them that the goal shouldn't be to reduce the standards for some, but to raise everyone else to the highest possible level.

This had struck me as universal wisdom. Now, rather than buy his crew new jackets, this ship's captain wanted mine to stop wearing them, and I wasn't going to let it happen. He could have tried to have me fired, but that was a chance I was willing to take.

That command master chief delivered my message and returned half an hour later with a new directive: "My CO has decided you can wear your jackets after all."

That ship could have bought those jackets, but never did. Meanwhile, the so-called *Benfold* Jacket became the rage, and my squadron commander ordered them for the five other ships under his command.

Jealousy and envy are powerful emotions and, if acted upon, can cause serious problems. Leaders must always watch out for them. A jealous commander may behave in ways that inhibit and soon paralyze his or her subordinates, who eventually turn off and tune out. The antidote lies in trying to make the people who work for you feel needed and highly valued. Help them believe in that wonderful old truism, "A rising tide lifts all boats." With perhaps a few exceptions, every organization's success is a collective achievement.

BUILD UP YOUR BOSSES.

I could not have succeeded by acting as a self-promoting careerist. Nothing alienates a boss faster than people who suck up, thirst for his or her job, or both. My mind-set was quite different: I aimed to be the consummate team player, a loyal servant to harassed bosses, whose needs I would anticipate before they even realized they had them. In the language of business, I would be a master of customer service.

What my admiral and commodore needed most, I decided, was a self-reliant ship commander who accomplished whatever needed to be done without being micromanaged. They wanted me (or any other skipper under their command) to supply a whole series of fleet-wide "bests." We would be the best-engineered ship, the best Tomahawk weapon provider, have the best search-and-seizure team, and the best retention rate for skilled sailors. And we would come in under budget.

It seemed crucial that I step up to the plate and swing for these things without being prompted or pressured. I rarely asked permission. I just acted on the theory that my bosses had authorized me to do so in their behalf. They wanted me to take care of things without being nagged. They had far too many other crises and problems. If I got my unit operating independently and delivering outstanding results, they could concentrate on other issues and do their jobs better—that's what any boss wants, as well as bragging rights.

My immediate boss, the commodore, was just the beginning of what turned out to be a growth market for our services. The Persian Gulf situation offered numerous opportunities because the crisis with Saddam brought me more customers—that is, more bosses: two more commodores and a senior captain, who in turn reported to no fewer than three admirals.

Despite being the most junior commanding officer in the entire Persian Gulf, I wanted to be part of the decision-making apparatus. I needed to glean as much influence as possible so that I could shortstop stupid policies in their infancy. I established individual relationships with each boss. For example, *Benfold* got to the Gulf three weeks before Captain Bob Moeller arrived to run air defense for the entire area, and we made it our business to learn what his needs would be. I sent him an e-mail introducing myself, telling him I was at his service, and suggesting issues he might think about. Keeping the correspondence private, I didn't send copies to the admirals or draw attention to myself. In this way, Moeller didn't feel threatened; he understood that I was interested only in improving the way we did business.

While he and his cruiser were crossing the Indian Ocean, I sent him personal messages telling him what he could expect when he reached the Gulf. I did this to improve our processes, not to gain credit. I wanted him to look good, and, most important, I wanted to be able to influence his decisions.

Normally, air defense commanders make judgments with minimal input, but since I had nurtured our relationship, he trusted me and was interested in my opinions. And he took my advice. This model worked so well he included the other COs in the process. As a result, the effectiveness of our air defense in the Gulf increased enormously. He looked good, and he was generous in sharing the credit with us. Had I acted intrusively or as though I had a personal agenda, I would have been shut out. Instead, I got a seat at the table when my bosses made decisions.

The same happened with Commodore Mike Duffy, who ran

the search-and-seizure operation. He had extremely high expectations and shared his pain when let down. Still, he learned to love *Benfold,* because we had also preceded him to the Gulf, scouted the search-and-seizure picture, and very privately sent him useful ideas for improving the process. He was pretty tough and demanding. We presented honest information in a nonthreatening way. If he ignored our recommendations, we didn't go around him. We stopped; the customer is always right. He grew to value our relationship.

Duffy admired *Benfold*'s computerized database that speeded up the process of merchant ship inspections, distributed copies throughout the fleet, and didn't contradict anyone who thought it was all his idea. That was fine with me. Credit wasn't my goal. I wanted to be known as a team player, focused on making the Navy better—Captain Indispensable of the USS *Go-To.*

We also made a lot of grateful friends among staff officers—the immediate aides of the admirals, commodores, and captains. Staff members in any organization have a tough job: They are under the gun to produce results, but usually have limited resources. By privately helping them, we made them look good to their bosses—a win/win deal that moved them to praise *Benfold,* which enhanced both its reputation and responsibilities.

When we got to the Gulf, the Pentagon imposed strict new requirements for arming and firing Tomahawks. Basically, the brass wanted the process speeded up. Ships with fewer and simpler missions than *Benfold* had trouble meeting the new deadlines. Why were we much faster than everyone else? Because our sailors sat down together, read all the pertinent publications, learned how all the equipment worked, and then devised innovative ways to meet the requirements. We sent a ten-page message to the other ships explaining our methods, which became standard operating procedure in the Persian Gulf. In fact, the entire Navy soon adopted them.

The United States and its allies profited from our work, but the biggest beneficiary was my boss, Vice Admiral Fargo. Had he been forced to tell the Pentagon that his ships could not meet the stringent new missile requirements, he would indeed have looked bad. Instead, his fleet aced the challenge—and that made him extremely appreciative.

It was our habit to assume initiative and give our customers the best service imaginable. That's why the Navy's war plan for the Gulf assigned the most difficult missions to us.

EXPECT THE BEST FROM YOUR CREW. YOU WILL GET IT.

In the fall of 1997, we were in the Persian Gulf. I was incredibly proud of my crew's growth and performance, and I had numerous measures to prove it. Still, the better I got to know them, the more convinced I became of their almost unlimited potential.

How much brainpower does the Navy—or any organization, for that matter—waste because those in charge don't recognize the full potential hiding at the low end of the hierarchy? If we stopped pinning labels on people and stopped treating them as if they were stupid, they would perform better. Why not instead assume that everyone is inherently talented, and then spur them to live up to those expectations? Too idealistic? On the contrary, that's exactly how *Benfold* became the best damn ship in the U.S. Navy.

It is also the way leaders in every kind of organization can achieve new levels of success—by encouraging the people working for them to express themselves on both a personal and a professional level.

Benfold is a warship whose bottom line is combat readiness. That the military is an organization that many young people join to escape from bad situations at home, such as drugs or gangs, may present a particular challenge to achieving our goal. Although these kids know that they don't want the lives they left behind, they don't yet know what they *do* want.

Getting such people to contribute in a meaningful way requires prodigious training and discipline. It also requires leaders who understand and appreciate them as individuals. A captain willing to do that gains a whole ship full of willing allies in the never-ending pursuit of combat readiness.

One of the fringe benefits of all my one-on-one interviewing was the insight it gave me into each sailor's life. Nothing was more useful—and moving—than learning why a kid had joined the Navy, and whether he or she had dreams or was just drifting. Most of my sailors had never had this kind of attention. No one in authority, let alone a ship captain, had ever sat down with them, discussed their goals, and helped them devise a plan to reach them.

I soon discovered a fascinating fact: About 50 percent of my young men and women signed up because their parents could not afford to send them to college. They wanted to take advantage of the GI Bill and save some money for living expenses when they got to school. When I asked them if they had done the preparatory work, forty-five of them said they had never taken the Scholastic Aptitude Test (SAT). Why not? Because their guidance counselors, teachers, and parents had decided they would never make it to college.

Struck by this, I directed my second in command to find an SAT administrator and fly him or her to the ship. As usual, he looked at me as if I had a hole in my head. But somehow he succeeded, and one Saturday afternoon, thirty miles south of Iraq, forty-five of my sailors took the SATs. When the results came back, one of the women had a combined score of 1490, good enough to get into most Ivy League colleges. She certainly topped my score when I entered Annapolis, and I had taken the test twice.

The response to our SAT session was so great that we took advantage of a Navy program that enabled sailors to take college courses via CD-ROM—they studied a lesson, took an exam, and wrote a paper that they sent back to the instructor. I soon had more than a hundred sailors enrolled. Another sixty-eight took math-refresher courses as well as the college-prep English that their high schools had failed to give them.

I was convinced that whether they stayed in the Navy or not, all this learning was bound to improve our little piece of society. To my surprise, it spurred my sailors to keep taking other tests— Navy advancement tests—and *Benfold* soon had a promotion rate two and a half times the Navy average. By upgrading their skills, the crew accomplished all sorts of things. We challenged their minds, which made shipboard life more fun. They boosted their chances of getting good jobs in the civilian economy, removing the specter of flipping burgers from their futures. And they clearly enriched the ship's skills pool, which in turn improved readiness.

I know business is tough, and bosses don't have the time or resources to play guidance counselor to troubled or underprivileged employees. Every manager and every company has limits on what it can and will do. But please consider my experience carefully. A lot of it is organizational attitude and mind-set. Anything you can do to understand your people, support them in tough times, and nurture their gifts will pay benefits to your bottom line.

BUILD A STRONG, DEEP BENCH.

When I took command of *Benfold*, I discovered that the usual policy was to have only one crew member able to perform each job: one job, one person. As a result, we were one-deep in just about every critical position. In effect, I was held hostage by the key people on the ship. If they left for any reason, I would have to scramble to get the job done, and probably not done well. It was very disconcerting.

I started training backups right away, and kept at it for my entire two years aboard *Benfold*. Not everyone loved that side of me, but being loved wasn't my priority.

The trip back to San Diego from the Persian Gulf took six weeks, and the crew set sail in R&R mode, as they had worked hard for the last hundred days. People understandably envisioned a leisurely cruise from port visit to port visit along the way. For the first twenty-four hours, I allowed this mood to prevail: We relaxed, had a cookout, and just hung out. Next day, we hit the training trail, using a new program designed to speed the learning process.

We drilled every day. People grumbled. They felt it was their right to do nothing for the six-week transit home. I announced that intense training was mandatory, period. I told them there was a choice—we could do it now or do it back in San Diego, when they would rather be at the beach with their families—and I chose now.

We not only kept our skills honed, we started training the third, fourth, and fifth string. When one team became proficient, we put in the second; when that team learned, in went the third. Soon, I was four- or five-deep in just about every position on that ship.

Cross-training became our mantra. By the time we reached San Diego, we had young sailors, barely out of boot camp, doing the jobs of first-class petty officers with several hash marks, and doing them well. By grooming people to move up and accept more responsibility, cross-training raised morale. By teaching them what their shipmates did, it improved team skills and spirit. The result was a huge plus for the ship.

Back in San Diego, we stood down for thirty days while the sailors took fifteen-day leaves, half the crew at a time. Then we headed out to sea for a three-week training cruise monitored by a team of outside experts. Their job was to assess our readiness for the next deployment. Ships, it seems, are always being assessed.

Instead of putting our first or second team in the watch stations, we put in our third or fourth string. These people were our future, likely to be on the ship for the next four or five years. So it paid great dividends for us to show the experts how well they performed.

And perform they did. According to the assessors, our third- and fourth-string teams were better than 90 percent of other ships' first-stringers. The assessors were amazed at *Benfold*'s proficiency and readiness, both short- and long-term, and said it was obvious that we had put enormous effort into training. For me, it was all a huge relief—the struggle had paid off.

My crew felt a different relief. They were just glad it was over.

COUNSEL CONTINUOUSLY—AND HONESTLY.

One of the most difficult tasks for any manager is counseling his or her employees at the yearly or semiannual evaluation. The Navy's annual evaluations can make or break a career. What worked best for me was to continuously counsel the people I was going to evaluate.

Unfortunately, we have to rank everyone against his or her peers, which can cause those ranked at the bottom to feel resentful. My advice is to remove the guesswork and let people know what the criteria are going to be, so they won't be surprised. Skipping this preparation only leads to heartache and discontent.

For my mid-level managers, my officers and chief petty officers, I set up clear and concise guidelines as to what I expected from them. I told them that I expected them to be experts in their own fields and that I would check on whether or not they were. Furthermore, they were expected to take on a project or two that would improve the ship's quality of life, or a military process that affected the entire organization. My theory is that when people see their contemporaries undertaking big projects, they will understand that doing so gets you a top evaluation. It's purely a matter of a person's own ambition. If you want to climb the ladder, you have to do more than your specific job; you have to do things that affect the lives of others in the organization.

The key to a successful evaluation is whether or not your people are surprised the day you give them their grades. If they're surprised, then clearly you have not done a good job of setting their expectations and providing feedback throughout the entire year. If you're communicating expectations and feedback on a continuous basis throughout the year, you will minimize, if not eliminate, people's surprise when you give them the final evaluation.

I gave consistent feedback at regular intervals throughout the year, formally on a quarterly basis, but also as part of the daily routine. Whenever people did something great, I let them know. Whenever they came up short, I did not let it fester until the end of the evaluation period; I got it out in the open right away. More than anything else, your people appreciate honesty from you. Even if they're doing something poorly, it's better to get it on the table early in the process so they have time to fix it. That's the key to being a good leader: ongoing counseling and consistent honesty.

No one likes being involved in an adversarial or confrontational situation, but from time to time it's inevitable. That's why we get paid the big bucks. Don't try to hide behind anyone else. Stand up to the plate.

When it is time to inform the bottom performers that, in fact, that's what they are, I have found that asking them how they would rate their own performances is effective. Most recognize that in relation to their peers, they are at the bottom of the curve.

Whenever I had deficient performers, I always laid out a game plan for them to improve. I'd bring them in, tell them what their problems were, what they needed to do to correct them, and provide training if they needed it. I would give them a deadline by which I expected them to have their deficiencies corrected. If necessary, I would clearly lay out in advance what would happen if they didn't.

I'm proud that I didn't have to fire or reassign anyone, but I was prepared to do so if I had to. All managers must be ready to shed poor performers, but only after you have given them a chance; you must be open and honest with them, clarify their deficiencies and how they can overcome them. And finally, you must spell out the stick: what will happen if they don't address those problems in a timely manner.

I went through that process with Lieutenant Jason Michal, who came to *Benfold* as chief engineer, one of the most critical positions on the ship. He was enormously talented and had been chief engineer on USS *Reid*, where he had developed a reputation as a fire breather. I was very concerned about him, because I didn't want him to ruin the atmosphere we had created on the ship.

First I gave him a break: Since he had spent the previous Christmas away from his family because he was on deployment to the Persian Gulf, I modified his training to let him have Christmas at home and meet us in Australia. The officer he was relieving had been on *Benfold* for three years and was burned out. The chief engineer may be the most demanding of the five department-head jobs, and their tour is only supposed to be eighteen months. The Navy was critically short of engineers at the time, so the tour length jumped to thirty-six months. The previous engineer desperately wanted to get his master's degree at the Navy's Postgraduate School in Monterey, California; the program began in September, and he had to be there if he was going to join it. Even though it meant that I would be at sea for almost a hundred days without a chief engineer, I decided to take the leap and let him go in September even though Jason Michal would not arrive until after Christmas. Most people thought I was crazy. But I decided it was the right thing to do. The added benefit was that it would allow me to entrust an ensign, Tom Holcomb, to step up and be the interim chief engineer. To be in a position like this as an ensign is unheard of in the Navy, and Tom did exactly what I thought he would do. He rose to the occasion and did a superb job. The bonus? When Jason finally arrived, I had two officers fully capable of filling the post.

When Jason showed up in Australia, he came to see me within two hours. He announced that he didn't agree with my leadership style, that it would not work with engineers because they need to be kicked in the butt instead of led. He said he could not operate under *Benfold*'s conditions.

It boggled my mind. I just could not believe anyone would have the audacity to say something like that on day one, just reporting to work. After recovering from my shock, I told him that, oh yes, he could achieve those results on this ship, and that I expected him to do just that. I also told him what would happen to him if he didn't: I would kick him off the ship, with a fitness report that would send him to repair diesels in the Aleutian Islands.

That got his attention, but it took him a while to actually understand and believe that what he had heard was actually true. He had been on the ship for about a week when we suffered a major engineering casualty. When he ran to the central control station, he found no officers or chief petty officers there. Traditionally, any problem could be solved if you threw enough officers and chiefs at it. He passed the word for his top two assistants, Master Chief Mike Nail and Ensign Tom Holcomb, to report to him, and when they did, he berated them for not being there in an emergency.

Master Chief Nail told him the facts of life on *Benfold,* and that the crew felt ownership of their work. "What do you want me to do, fix it myself?" Mike said. "That's what we pay these people to do. We have trained them. They can fix it. It would be demotivating for them if I had to go down and fix every casualty. It also would never prepare us for success."

It shocked Jason Michal that his master chief would talk to him this way. Even more shocking was the fact that some of the lowest-ranking people in his department fixed a major breakdown. His world was rocked, too, because I wasn't standing over his shoulder demanding a status report every five minutes. I didn't need to be because I knew that the engineers felt ownership of the ship and would do their best to fix it. They knew I was concerned and wanted to be informed, but they also knew that I would wait for them to tell me.

Jason will say that that was one of the biggest lessons he learned. He started realizing that you can actually lead engineers and treat them with respect. And he became one of the best officers and leaders I have ever seen. Words cannot possibly convey what a truly phenomenal leader he became.

CHAPTER TEN

GENERATE UNITY

⚓ ONE OF MY HARDER TASKS WAS GETTING PEOPLE TO AC-
cept that we were all (in this case literally) in the same
boat. Either we would support one another or the whole ship
could be in critical trouble that no one could escape.

One of the toughest things for organizations to accomplish is
to get people to set aside personal differences and work for the
good of everyone involved. I don't care to have the best weapons
department of any ship in the Navy if the engineers can't make
the propeller turn and get us to the battle. If that's the case, we
are one of the worst ships. The task of the leader is to assemble
the best team possible, train it, then figure out the best way to get
the members to work together for the good of the organization.

After I had been with the secretary of defense for about a year, we returned from an overseas trip and were critiquing what we had accomplished. I summoned up the courage to inquire why he had hired me in the first place. "Why did you choose me over those most highly qualified candidates?" I asked. Dr. Perry responded, "Mike, I have been in both government and business for over forty years. I can hire the smartest people around. But I have found what works the best is a staff that works together and backstops each other. The staff decided that you were the one they could work with the best."

Perhaps the most malignant obstacle to forming a cohesive unit is also the U.S. military's worst-kept secret: its inability to end racial and gender discrimination. Contrary to Pentagon hopes and hype, racism persists and sexual harassment is pandemic in nearly every military unit, land, sea, or air. In fact, this shouldn't be surprising. The military, like any organization, reflects the larger culture of which it is a part.

Treating people with dignity and respect is not only morally right, but also highly practical and productive. Unity became the fundamental purpose of my leadership model. We achieved that goal because we learned how to make people want to belong to our 310-member club, ready to give their best to a fair-dealing ship that clearly valued them, no matter what color or sex they were.

FORGET DIVERSITY. TRAIN FOR UNITY.

Shortly after I took command of *Benfold,* I set out to find out exactly how dreadful the climate on the ship was. I decided to read the portion of a survey that addressed what people of different

169

ethnic groups thought about one another. In the spirit of endorsing equal opportunity, these mandatory surveys are part of the status report that an outgoing commander hands over to his or her successor.

I asked for the results. Turns out that they didn't shine a very favorable light on an aspect of the ship's operations. As such, no one was too keen to talk about the survey. But it's been my experience in management that while good news makes you feel warm inside, it's the negative news that makes you learn and helps improve your performance at your job.

Among the various issues that were brought up, a big one dealt with the sailors' perceptions. Some women felt there was sexual harassment on the ship, some minorities felt there was racial prejudice, and some white males even felt there was favoritism toward women and minorities. That's a trifecta that's tough to overcome.

My first move was to cancel our diversity training program. I could have been fired for that, but in my view it was common sense that any program that produced such awful results was clearly ineffective. I had no intention of allowing anything ineffective on *Benfold*.

In its place I substituted unity training, concentrating on people's likenesses and our common goals rather than differences. Unity begins by recognizing common interests. A ship of 310 people who looked and acted just like me would probably be one of the worst ships in the history of the Navy. If you surround yourself with people exactly like yourself, you run the dangerous risk of groupthink, and no one has the creativity to come up with new ideas. The goal is not to create a group of clones, culturally engineered to mimic one another. Rather, unity is about maximizing uniqueness and channeling that toward the common goals of the group. Too often individuals champion their individuality as an excuse to do whatever they want, whenever they want. That is no formula for success in battle or in business. As Benjamin Franklin put it when he defied the British and signed the Declaration of Independence on July 4, 1776, "We must indeed all hang together, or, assuredly, we shall all hang separately."

In some ways, I base unity training on the awful example of the Washington Redskins in 1996, when the team fielded a jumble of highly talented, overpaid individuals who looked like Super Bowl champions, but won only a few games all season. Fast-forward to the year 2000: The Redskins had the highest payroll in the National Football League, but still could not make it to the playoffs. What I wanted was what the Redskins needed and Franklin inspired: a team of highly talented individuals that played as one.

Unity training was one of the few programs I chose not to delegate; I conducted it myself. I reached out to each of the ship's twenty-four divisions and told them how I felt. First, there was no place for racial or gender prejudice on *Benfold*. To deny their existence would be foolish, but to let such attitudes show on my ship was anathema to everything it stood for and grounds for immediate and severe disciplinary action. I also led with those very same values. All too often, our words say one thing and our actions quite another.

There is no such thing as a truly level playing field, I told them, but we were going to work damn hard to make ours as fair as possible. Everyone has strengths and weaknesses; no one is perfect, including the commanding officer. I would applaud their strengths and help them overcome their weaknesses, but above all, I wanted them to treat one another with dignity and respect. And though we all want to win at whatever we do, the important point was *how* we won—whether we did it in a way that made us proud or ashamed, bigger or smaller. In short, how we got there was just as important as getting there. And if I could stay proud of whatever I did, I told them, so could they, making *Benfold* a great ship in the process. In my interviews with the crew, I also asked if there was any sexual harassment or racial prejudice being expressed on board. And when I heard about an occurrence, I acted immediately. If you don't intend to act, then don't bother to ask if it is going on. It will only make matters worse.

One complicating factor, which is going to take years to overcome, is that the Navy officer corps is composed overwhelmingly of white males, while the enlisted men and women include blacks, Latinos, Asian Americans, and other minorities. Inevitably, this was the case on *Benfold,* too. That's the struggle every institution faces. Fortunately, most organizations are finally waking up to the fact that management needs to reflect the makeup of the workforce.

This isn't a starry-eyed ideal but a hard, cold business fact. People need to know that their interests are being represented at the top. More important, people need positive role models, such as William Perry provided for me. It is naive to assume that race and gender play no part in determining who our role models are. There are numerous ships in the Navy today wherein the officer corps is made up entirely of white males. This single fact is keeping those ships from being as good as they possibly can be. I was extremely fortunate that the random personnel generator at the Bureau of Naval Personnel handed me an officer and a chief petty officer corps that reflected the makeup of the crew. It inspired members of the crew to think such a position was possible for them.

Little by little, the crew began to buy into my perspective, especially when they saw me backing up my words with actions. We started to improve a little. And I kept walking around the ship, questioning the crew, drawing them out. I'm a big believer in getting resentments and grumbling out in the open, where they can do a lot less damage.

Those conversations helped, and so did my efforts to chip away at ingrained behaviors that stem from the military's hierarchy. By such gestures as joining the enlisted people at cookouts, having lunch once a week with the crew on the mess decks, and making sure visiting VIPs got to talk to the crew, I tried to show the officers that in human terms we were all in this together, and each person was indispensable to the unity of the *Benfold* team.

To me, diversity training had merely made people more aware of their *differences*. Our unity training focused on *common* interests and positive reasons to value others instead of a top-down prohibition against devaluing them. It was the difference between being rewarded for good behavior and being punished for bad behavior. In this case, the reward was to become a full-scale shareholder in the *Benfold* community, with all the rights and privileges that membership brought.

The payoff was reflected in our equal-opportunity surveys. When I departed, only 3 percent of minorities on board reported any type of racial prejudice, and just 3 percent of women reported sexual harassment. Of course, that is still 6 percent too many, but it was a quantum improvement over the overwhelming percentage who had previously reported favoritism, sexual harassment, and racial prejudice.

Benfold became a more enlightened ship, but not because I gave long lectures scolding sailors for their racial and gender prejudices. People changed because we proved the benefits of community. They changed because in their hearts, these sailors wanted and needed to belong to a team that cared for its members at least as well as it cared for its cutting-edge machinery. For the most part, these feelings had never been spoken on *Benfold* until I voiced them. Articulating the feelings that your people are afraid to speak is a large part of what leaders, including ship captains, do for a living.

DEAL OUT PUNISHMENT STRICTLY BUT FAIRLY.

Three months after taking command, before I initiated my effort to eliminate racism and sexism on board, I had a disciplinary case that proved a crucible for my unity training program. We were in Bahrain when a very serious racist incident occurred.

Some of my sailors were returning on a Navy bus from an evening of drinking on the base. Two black sailors were singing a loud rap song that included the word "nigger." Two white sailors yelled at them to shut up because, according to the white sailors and others on the bus, they were annoying everyone. They didn't stop. When they all got off the bus, hot words were exchanged all the way back to the ship, with one of the white sailors using the N-word. Then a big fight broke out in quarters, during which one sailor threatened to kill another. Eventually, thirteen people were involved in trying to break up the brawl. The two black and one white sailor were charged with assault.

For me, this was a pivotal event. As the leader in a crisis, I knew that everyone in the organization was watching me very closely, searching for signals that would reveal my priorities. A leader's every action is always scrutinized, and I knew that everything I did in this most difficult case would quickly spread throughout the ship. I knew, too, that my actions would influence the crew's behavior as well as the ship's culture for months, if not longer.

As the ship's commander, I was in many ways the court of last resort. When a Navy person breaks an important rule or regulation, he or she is in violation of the Uniform Code of Military Justice, the Navy's equivalent of civilian criminal law. The accused is placed on report and brought before "captain's mast," a hearing in which the captain functions as judge, jury, and executioner. After an investigation to determine the facts, the captain takes over, and I do mean takes over.

It is the captain alone who interrogates the defendant, cross-examines the witnesses, determines guilt or innocence, and decides on acquittal or conviction. For punishment, the captain is authorized to throw miscreants out of the Navy, refer them to a higher military court ashore, restrict them to the ship with onerous duties for forty-five days, cut their pay in half for two months, reduce them in rank, or even lock them up in the brig on a diet of bread and water for three days.

In itself, the captain's power is appropriate. Captains have always needed autocratic powers to deal with mutinous sailors. And for sailors in peril on the sea, having someone clearly in charge tends to be comforting.

The question, of course, is whether a captain can use this power in ways that win the crew's respect and trust. Neither tyrants nor pushovers have a chance. The best skippers blend fairness and strength, and they learn from life, not just from a book.

In this case, the two black sailors had been in trouble before. Earlier in my career, multiple disciplinary proceedings would have been enough reason to throw them out of the Navy immediately. This time, however, I asked Master Chief Scheeler what he could tell me about these sailors to help me understand why they acted this way.

I learned that they were both from the inner city of Detroit. One had a father in prison, and the other had never met his father. Both their mothers were on welfare. That didn't excuse them, but it put events in another light—and gave me an opportunity. I thought of my own childhood, growing up with two caring parents in a small town in Pennsylvania. It seemed clear that neither of these young men had a positive male role model, and I started to wonder if I could handle this situation in a way that offered them a different experience. This would depend on their behavior and what I learned and did in the initial hearing.

Thus far, everyone involved had been lying. The white sailors didn't want to admit that one of them had muttered the word "nigger" in the confrontation, and the black sailors didn't want to admit they had used the word, too, as part of their rap song. I needed the truth, so I sweated it out of them—literally.

The hearing was in a room much too small for the sixty witnesses who were crammed into it. I turned off the air-conditioning and started asking questions. It got hot, and then hotter. Three hours later, one sailor cracked and told me exactly what had happened. Once the dam broke, everyone turned honest.

I asked the two black sailors if they wanted to stay in the Navy. "Yes, definitely," each of them answered.

"Okay," I said. "I'm going to throw the book at you, only if you want to stay. One more violation, though, gets you an e-ticket out of the Navy." The white sailor was a punk, and I startled the entire room by calling him such. All by himself, he could have avoided this whole sorry drama, and I wanted everyone on that ship to know that I knew that. I wanted them to know that I expect people to walk away if they can. I sentenced them and the white sailor who had been involved in the fight to the maximum punishment, short of dishonorable discharge: I restricted all three to the ship for forty-five days, gave them forty-five days of extra duty, and put them on half pay for two months.

The whole process was draining. Nothing in my training had ever prepared me for this. I was in totally uncharted territory and I knew that this one case could make or break my tour as CO. I walked back up to my cabin, completely exhausted and drenched in sweat. I felt we had just successfully navigated through a minefield. Much like many black people in civilian society, the black members of the crew felt they were being discriminated against. Unbeknownst to me at the time, this would be the last disciplinary proceeding involving a young black male for the next twenty-seven months, marking a dramatic decline in offenses. Did we have a policy that said "turn a blind eye toward any violations by black males"? Hardly. In fact, we tightened the standards for everyone.

What explains the dramatic decline? Unity and the fact that our values determined how we led. Those young black men on *Benfold* were also here prior to my arrival. Only now did they have as level a playing field as possible. Instead of restraining people, we strengthened them. And we provided a positive model for all to emulate.

I met with Master Chief Scheeler. "I just tore those three sailors down," I said. "Now it's your job to start building them back up. I want you to redeem these kids."

Master Chief Scheeler called them into his office and said, "You know what? You're on the captain's shit list. You can stay on it and suffer, if that's your choice. Or you can get off and become responsible citizens, in which case here's what you need to do." He worked with the two black sailors every day, while First-Class Petty Officer John Rafalko and Chief Petty Officer Janice Harris supervised the white sailor. They both spent an enormous amount of time coaching him and setting an example for him. This mentoring process was becoming so successful that it was rolled out as a preventive measure to every crew member who was close to being in trouble.

One night at sea, I saw the two sailors that Master Chief Scheeler was supervising, so I asked Scheeler to join me in challenging them to a game in the mess decks after dinner. Naturally, they accepted. People walking through the mess decks were flabbergasted when they saw the four of us sitting around playing cards. We gave these young men big-man status, and we were sending a message of forgiveness and acceptance. I felt it was my privilege to support these men. They turned around completely and became stars among their peers. Both were promoted and both continue to do well. It is possible that if I had thrown them out of the Navy, they would have ended up in the criminal justice system. A year later, the white sailor asked me to reenlist him for another tour in the Navy. I was sitting in my chair on the bridge wing and asked him if he could have envisioned this a year ago when I called him a punk. "No way," he responded. But he was no longer a punk. He had matured into a fine young man.

This experience taught me—and the whole crew, I hope—two valuable lessons. The first was the importance of taking people's background and circumstances into consideration before passing judgment on them. Not everyone starts out at the same place, but with half a chance and some direction, most people left behind will catch up fairly quickly. The second was the significance of helping wrongdoers become better citizens, instead of discarding them, as our society too often does. The effort we're putting into building prisons should be used instead to redeem people.

I was determined to move away from the zero-defect mentality that, in my view, is a cancer spreading through too many organizations, including the military. I wanted people who screwed up on my ship to know two things: First, they will be appropriately punished; second, they will get another chance.

WHAT'S BAD FOR WOMEN IS BAD FOR YOUR SHIP.

The Navy was trying to change its attitude toward women as well as blacks. *Benfold*, for example, was one of the first Navy ships built from the keel up to accommodate women. But the failure of the diversity training program suggested that female-fit quarters, although important, were not the primary issue. They did little or nothing to change hearts and habits.

This was underscored by the resentment that our sister ship, USS *Stethem*, felt toward us. It angered that crew enormously that even though *Stethem* performed well, *Benfold* always performed better. Though we looked like twins, the ships were very different in spirit and achievement. For one thing, *Stethem* had an all-male crew, and some of its sailors derisively referred to the ships as "his and hers." Frustrated by our superior performance, *Stethem*'s sailors were constantly searching for something to beat us at, but in our view we had another advantage: We were a mixed-gender ship.

We encountered the same reaction when we got to the Persian Gulf in 1997. The Joint Chiefs of Staff ordered the aircraft carrier *George Washington* to join the *Nimitz* in the area. She brought two escorts with her, *Normandy* and *Carney*.

The captain of *Carney* was an outstanding officer and had been XO of *Shiloh* when I relieved him in 1993. We had a friendly professional rivalry. If you picture Popeye, you will get a sense of him—an old salt who loves the sea and always has a sea story at the ready. He took a great deal of pride in calling his crew "the *Carney* men"—the ship had an all-male crew.

Though he ran a great ship, *Benfold*'s performance was better— heck, in my opinion, in terms of morale and enthusiasm, *Benfold* was better. In the Gulf, *Carney*'s crew members didn't do as well on Tomahawk tests. They were very good, but were not at our level.

Vice Admiral Fargo directed *Benfold* to write a report detailing how we met the requirements of firing the Tomahawks. We were happy to do so, but it may have irked *Carney*'s captain, who, along with his crew, had been bested by a mixed-gender ship.

I had given a lot of thought to the role of women in the Navy, because the military is being pulled apart at the seams over the issue of integrating men and women into combat roles. I was determined from day one that women would be accepted on *Benfold*. A ship, just like an office or a factory, is a workplace, where no sexual harassment is tolerated.

Obviously, there are some jobs that women physically can't do, but those are relatively few—and, truth be told, many men can't do them either. For example, when the USS *Cole* was the target of a terrorist bomb that blew a hole in her side, the ship nearly sunk. One of the required tasks to keep her afloat was to use wooden beams, which we store on the ship, to "shore up," or keep the underwater hull from collapsing. These beams are extraordinarily heavy and you are working in a partially flooded space. It requires tremendous physical strength to maneuver them into place. Even some of the men could not have muscled the beams into place. But with everyone working as a team, each person contributing their part, they did a remarkable, no, a heroic job in saving their ship. The women sailors, I found, were every bit as motivated, if not more, when it came to achieving great results.

I didn't set out to turn *Benfold* into a sociology lab. This was about combat readiness. The Navy is faced with a limited labor pool, and to exclude any portion of the population is just plain stupid. The Navy was staffed at 80 percent of its ideal strength, and a quarter of all new recruits are women. We could not get the ships out of port if we didn't accept women.

After doing our best to bring *Carney* men up to snuff, we left the Gulf and, in late January 1998, pulled into Melbourne, Australia, where city security guards keep watch over the piers. One midnight, I came back from a night on the town and the guard stopped me to ask, "What's wrong with your crew?" Since I wasn't sure what he was getting at, I said, "Come again, mate?" He said he had never seen a better-behaved or more disciplined crew than the one aboard *Benfold*. He said he usually saw only drunken sailors who were rowdy and difficult. I thanked him and beamed with pride.

He was right, of course, and in my view it was because we had women on board who we truly accepted as part of the crew. We didn't have the gender integration problems wracking the rest of the military, for one reason: We treated everyone with respect and dignity, and required the same from our people. Once again, it was simply the right thing to do, but it also had a definite salutary effect on the crew's manners and behavior. Having accepted the women as equals, the men did not want to be shown up by them. Not only did their performance improve, they were also forced to grow up and stop being juvenile.

The base commander in Bahrain—the first female base commander in the Middle East—was understandably skeptical about *Benfold*'s claim to gender equality, and came aboard to see for herself. Lo and behold, she found no credibility—or gender— gap. Our women, who ranked from seaman to lieutenant, were all doing phenomenally well. We had no fraternization cases that you hear so much about from the media. The base commander interviewed women sailors on every deck, from stem to stern, and they all said the same thing: They loved serving on *Benfold*.

I served with a lot of fine officers in my career, but my navigator, Lieutenant Jennifer Ellinger, was one of the best. *Benfold* was the junior ship when USS *Gary* and USS *Harry W. Hill* were deployed. Traditionally, the senior ships plot the course to and from the Persian Gulf, but because their crews were less competent, Jennifer steered us there and back. She performed superbly. In addition, she was the best second baseman I have ever seen on an officers' softball team. I could always count on her to get a hit when we needed one. Unfortunately, most of the male officers on the team were not as reliable. It was my dumb luck to have a group of officers who could not smack the ball out of the infield, so they never beat the chief petty officers' team. This was one of my biggest disappointments in my two years on *Benfold*. It was also one of Jennifer's, since she is as competitive as I.

In the business world, there is a myth that women have achieved equality, when in fact a great deal of subtle harassment and discrimination still exists. Men resent competing with women for their jobs. In society at large, we have disturbing cultural trends, such as superstar rappers who advocate violence against women. I think we can all learn from *Benfold*'s experience.

I found some impressive fringe benefits to having women on board. The story of Third-Class Petty Officer Gussie Jones is just one example.

Gussie's chance to shine came because of *Benfold*'s program to give enlisted people the responsibility of being officer of the deck—the person in charge of the quarterdeck when the ship is in port. That person tends to security, logs in visitors, and keeps track of everything entering and leaving the ship. Since it is the visitor's first impression of the ship, the quarterdeck has always been a top priority; it's Navy tradition to tolerate no mistakes in what can be a hectic and demanding job, especially during busy shifts. For that reason, usually officers or chief petty officers stand this watch during the day. But I wanted to give junior people the satisfaction of handling more responsibility, and also to free up senior people for other jobs. *Benfold* began qualifying first- and second-class petty officers as officers of the deck.

They made some mistakes, which we corrected without berating them, but, in the long run, the program was such a success that other ships began copying it. We decided to go a step further and reach down to third-class petty officers.

Up stepped twenty-two-year-old Gussie Jones.

After she passed the qualification, she was scheduled to take the midnight watch—the quietest possible time. Nothing doing, I said; put her on from 0700 to noon, the busiest watch of the day. I wanted the rest of the ships to know that we had a third-class petty officer as the officer of the deck.

On Jones's very first watch, my new boss, Commodore Jim Stavridis, unexpectedly showed up. Gussie announced his arrival on the public-address system. In the Navy, arriving and departing senior officers are announced by their titles, not their names, and the number of bells suitable for their rank. Three- and four-star admirals get eight bells, one- and two-stars get six, and commodores get four. But harried, surprised, and nervous, Gussie gave Commodore Stavridis six bells and announced, "Destroyer Squadron Twenty-One . . . arriving."

Hearing this in my cabin, I knew she had made a mistake. I also knew that my boss had probably shown up. So I raced down to the quarterdeck just as my officers were getting there, and before anyone could say anything I grabbed the commodore by the arm, shook his hand, and with a big grin said, "Let *Benfold* be the first to predict your selection to rear admiral next year." A huge grin broke out on his face. Gussie was embarrassed, but not humiliated. And most important, I sent a message to my officers on how to treat people. (By the way, the commodore was indeed made a rear admiral a year later.)

Gussie's second watch was five days later. It was the noon to 4 P.M. watch on a cold, rainy, windy day in San Diego, and the ship across the pier was attempting to get under way. When a ship leaves a pier, sailors from nearby ships pitch in to help cast off the mooring lines, and some of our crew were called for this duty.

But the departing ship's officers were of the old "hurry up and wait" school. They had the line handlers muster up and then stand in the rain for forty-five minutes—while the officers were warm and dry in the pilot house. Then the ship developed an engineering problem, which prolonged the delay. So Gussie Jones called my command duty officer, Lieutenant K. C. Marshall, to the quarterdeck. When he arrived, she said the sailors had been standing in the rain for nearly an hour.

"Do you suppose we could bring them up here to stand under the awning to keep dry?"

"Absolutely," said K.C., and proceeded to get them coffee and hot chocolate from the *Benfold* café.

How is it that twenty-two-year-old Gussie Jones, standing her second watch, had the good judgment and common sense to bring those sailors out of the rain when the officers on the other ship did not?

CHAPTER ELEVEN

IMPROVE YOUR PEOPLE'S QUALITY OF LIFE

I OFTEN GET A FEELING THAT CORPORATE AMERICA, like the military, is headed for a nervous breakdown. We are now permanently wired to our work, wherever we are. Even on vacation, we're tethered to pagers, cell phones, and laptops, so we can log in from the beach. This is okay, in moderation. In excess, it eats away at the inner reservoir of spirit that people need to draw on when life gets tough. If you work seventy or eighty hours a week and never take time out for a work/life balance, the reservoir doesn't refill and soon you're running on empty. When times get tough, the body may be willing but the spirit will be out to lunch.

Long ago, one of Neptune's admirals must have decreed that working sailors are forbidden to have fun at sea. Our own admirals took the rule as gospel; no alternative had ever occurred to them. I wanted to change that. When I interviewed my sailors, I asked them not only how we could improve the ship's performance, but also how we could have fun at work. The responses were amazing.

FUN WITH YOUR FRIENDS
MAKES A HAPPY SHIP.

One sailor said it would be neat if we had a stereo system, and maybe once a week at sea we could gather on the flight deck and watch the sun set while listening to jazz. We did that. At sunset every Thursday, a big crowd collected—men and women, officers and enlisted ranks—to listen to jazz as the sea darkened, which certainly contributed to the glue that held that crew together.

Another sailor thought it would be fun if we could smoke cigars while we were out there listening to jazz and watching the sun go down. So we bought a humidor and laid in a supply of pretty good cigars. Thursday night duly became Jazz & Cigar Night on *Benfold*.

Yet another sailor suggested a happy hour every Friday night at sea. I was ready to break a lot of rules, but definitely not the one that bans serving alcohol on a ship at sea. Still, you can have happy hour without alcohol, or so I decreed. Every other Friday night, we gathered on the mess decks for a feast—steamship round, buffalo wings, the best available shrimp. We also bought a karaoke machine. I made two stipulations. The first, which the crew unanimously approved, was that the captain would not sing, or even try. The second, reflecting a cultural failing of mine, was that there would be no country music. I can't bear the stuff, even through Walkman earphones, let alone playing on a karaoke machine at destroyer-level volume. But people were polite about the captain's eccentricity. And it was wonderful to hear my sailors laughing as they sat together singing karaoke, especially without all the sobs, twangs, and wails that they loved and I loathed.

We tried to instill fun in everything we did, especially mundane, repetitive jobs such as loading food aboard the ship. Except in San Diego, where Irv Refkin's conveyor belt came to our aid, that was a chore we did by hand, and it was hard work. We decided that music would make the job go faster. With our huge stereo system playing great tunes, it was a whole new scene. Everyone danced and boogied to the music. The officers and chiefs supervising the workforce ended up pitching in themselves. Music seemed to make even the most boring task fun—a lesson that somehow escaped the U.S. Navy.

Still another sailor said, "Why don't we put a sheet on the back bulkhead on the flight deck and get a movie projector and show movies under the stars at night?" I thought it was a fantastic idea. Though we had put TVs and VCRs in every workspace, so people could watch movies on their own, the flight deck idea took us back to the time when we all watched movies on ships as a single audience and shared the experience together. The throwback seemed to me a step forward in unifying my crew.

So we had Saturday Night at the Drive-In. We were in the Persian Gulf, thirty miles south of Iraq, and we showed a double feature every Saturday night. The first film was always a comedy, the second an action-packed thriller. We provided three hundred bags of microwave popcorn, as well as sodas. People brought their beach chairs, blankets, and pillows, lay out under the stars, and watched a movie. Other ships sidled up and took positions a hundred yards off our flight deck, so that they, too, could watch.

The point was that having fun with your friends creates infinitely more social glue for any organization than stock options and bonuses will ever provide.

Having fun is a notion you can apply to any workplace anywhere. Not long ago, I proposed it to a conspicuously dour bank, and the managers looked alarmed. They said, more or less, "Fun isn't allowed here. It goes against the culture of the organization." But one of the managers broke ranks: "Why don't we have Laugh-In once a month?" she said. The others softened, albeit slowly, and the light finally dawned. So now, one day a month, the bank's once mirthless employees gather for a brown-bag lunch and sit together watching reruns of TV classics like *I Love Lucy* and *Gilligan's Island*. These people had barely said a word to one another for days, if not decades. The last I heard, they were actually laughing.

THE FIRST PRIORITY: GOOD FOOD.

My parents came to San Diego to watch me take command of *Benfold,* and afterward I invited them aboard for a six-hour cruise. It was their first time on a ship, let alone on a ship I commanded, and I wanted them to love it.

Unfortunately, when I took them for lunch in the officers'

mess, we discovered it was chicken-nuggets day. I don't know how you can ruin chicken nuggets, but these were hard, tasteless, and downright embarrassing. If this is what we were being fed in the officers' mess, I thought, what might my crew be eating?

Food is extremely important on a ship. For all the promise of excitement and adventure at sea, there's a lot of monotony in the Navy, with many days of rote performance and routine maintenance. Providing much more than subsistence, meals give people a chance to socialize and relax, and they provided me an opportunity to boost the crew's morale.

Every Navy ship has a menu review board. Once a month, each of the ship's divisions (*Benfold* has twenty-four) sends a representative to the board to talk about the menu. It often seems we have more meetings than we have people, and most divisions don't send their best to this one: Historically, it is a non-value-added event that was established for some reason that no one remembers but aren't allowed to cancel since we get inspected on it. I showed up, unannounced, at the next meeting.

On most ships, all hands stay alert to whatever the captain is doing, and word quickly spread that I was sitting in on the menu review board. Shocked, the two officers in charge of food who had not planned on attending showed up—and an earnest culinary discussion ensued. I listened and finally spoke up. "I have to tell you," I said, "the food on this ship stinks. What's the problem?"

Everyone was taken aback at my bluntness. But I wasn't out to berate or punish anyone; all I wanted was to understand why the food was so terrible. The menu review board is typically chaired by the chief petty officer who runs the enlisted mess decks. In this case, the chief volunteered that she had some cooks who didn't follow the menu cards. So I got all the cooks together and told them that they were key players in my campaign to boost morale. I stressed the importance of following the menu cards and said I wanted their support. I wanted to support the cooks as well as everyone else.

When I can build people up, their work improves, and my own morale leaps. My approach with the cooks was to walk through the galley just about every other day, telling them how much I appreciated their hard work. And the food got a lot better.

But with a limited palette of mostly inferior ingredients, the cooks alone could not solve the problem. I took my kitchen campaign a step further.

Ever since Moby Dick was a minnow, Navy ships have been required to get bids from food purveyors and buy only from the lowest bidder. What began as an anticorruption policy became a recipe for lousy food—unless, that is, you are fond of nameless peanut butter that comes in big aluminum cans and "beef" so fatty and tasteless that it's called "mystery meat" by the crew.

While I was in the Pentagon, my boss, Secretary of Defense William Perry, had fought hard to get Congress to pass the Federal Acquisition Reform Act, which freed military people from having to make all purchases according to government standards. Although this was good government in action, it got no play in the media. That law allowed us to buy supplies on the open market and become shrewd shoppers in the process. If I wanted Skippy peanut butter, I could buy it; if I wanted good steak, I could get the best cuts. I directed my supply officer to cut "cheap" out of his vocabulary and replace it with "quality." "Buy Skippy if that's what the crew wants," I said. "And make sure to ask if they want chunky or smooth." This is how I got the money to send six cooks to culinary school. *Benfold* ended up serving the best food in the Navy. Our Thanksgiving dinners were as good as the ones I had at home (sorry, Mom).

When I took command I had three top priorities: to get better food, implement better training, and make as many promotions as I could every year. Though some people titter when I list food as number one, the fact is that it raised morale and helped start the process of transforming our ship.

ADD TO YOUR CREW'S BOTTOM LINE.

In late August and September of 1997, we made our way from Hawaii to the Persian Gulf, with memorable stopovers in Singapore and Thailand. We spent thirty of those days at sea aggressively training in the use of Tomahawk cruise missiles. Tomahawks, which can travel over a thousand miles and land within feet of their target, are this country's primary artillery. I wanted the best deployment team in the Navy.

Our training paid off. *Benfold* was the only ship in our three-ship group that was Tomahawk-capable (*Hill* and *Gary* weren't configured to carry Tomahawks). The closer we got to the Gulf, the more provocative Saddam Hussein became; we were ordered to speed up, leave *Gary* and *Harry W. Hill* behind, and get our Tomahawks in position as quickly as possible.

The U.S. Navy doesn't issue rum to its warriors, but it does hand out incentive pay to those in harm's way, a region that then included the Persian Gulf. For being inside the Gulf, even for one minute of one day, a sailor's pay for that entire month would be tax-free.

Our orders only said to reach Bahrain on October 3, 1997, but, fortunately, they didn't tell us how to do so. With a speed of eighteen knots, we could make Bahrain as directed. However, I figured that a speed of twenty-four knots for two days straight would get us just inside the Gulf at 2359 on the night of September 30, giving us the last minute of the month inside the tax-free zone and adding at least $350 to each crew member's paycheck. Never mind that it required us to be so far ahead of schedule that we only needed to do five knots for the next two days to make it to Bahrain as directed. I could have gotten slapped hard if I had gotten caught.

As it happened, however, a new Iraqi crisis popped up on October 1, and Vice Admiral Fargo ordered us to the northern Gulf to help. No one ever thought to ask why *Benfold* was inside the Persian Gulf two days early.

So now it can be told: Saddam did us a favor. Thanks to his threats, we added value for our battle group commander, and my sailors got a bonus in addition to paying no taxes in the month of September.

IN HEAVY TIMES, LIGHTEN UP.

In early November 1997, we came very close to launching our Tomahawk missiles. It was a tense time. Kofi Annan, the United Nations secretary-general, was traveling around the Middle East trying to arrange a peace deal. Meanwhile, Saddam was threatening to throw out the UN weapons inspectors. We stood by, ready to shoot if the order came down. The media back home were making war sound inevitable.

Still, it was a beautiful fall in the Persian Gulf, and one Sunday afternoon, with the thermometer showing eighty degrees, I decided we needed a break from the crisis. *Benfold* carried two small Zodiac boats with outboard motors, and we organized a boat race, using floats to set up a course alongside the ship. Each of the ship's five departments entered a team, and we started the races by blowing the ship's whistle. Zodiacs are pretty fast—they can hit about forty miles an hour. To make the event even more festive, we had a cookout on the flight deck. My crew loved the whole thing, but the one who relished it most was the chaplain.

Lieutenant Glenn Woods was visiting us from the carrier *Nimitz*. He loved the difference between our ship and *Nimitz*, which had several full-time chaplains and psychiatrists to deal with the problems of its 5,500-person crew. As a sideline, they occasionally visited other ships to see if pastoral help was needed. We gave Woods an office on *Benfold* and announced his availability for troubled souls. But his only takers, he told me, were people who came to ask if he needed anything.

The chaplain got into the spirit of Zodiac racing. We put him in one of the boats as a crew member, and he refused to get out. He said he had never had as much fun in his whole Navy career. He was so delighted that I worried a bit about his sharing the story of our exploits when he got back to *Nimitz*. Technically, putting our boats in the water required clearance from Commodore Duffy. I told him that the boats needed maintenance work over the side, which was true. But I had not mentioned that racing would be part of the tune-ups.

As I suspected, the chaplain was too full of good spirits to keep the experience to himself. Back on *Nimitz,* word spread like wild-fire that even in these grave times, with war likely any day, *Benfold* was out having boat races. Sailors on the carrier said that if they ever got within five miles of *Benfold,* half of them would jump off and swim over because we were having such fun.

Duffy never mentioned the races.

LET THE CREW SHOW OFF THE SHIP.

Next, we went to Australia.

In every port, I ignored the elitist Navy rule that only "distin-guished" guests can visit a ship. I saw no reason to forbid my sailors to invite their newfound friends aboard. In fact, I encour-aged people to go out and make friends and do just that. Some-times when I saw a sailor showing his or her pals around, I joined them and helped explain how the ship worked.

My sailors made what seemed to me literally thousands of new friends, and I was struck by their eagerness to bring them aboard. They clearly felt enormous pride in *Benfold.* I often mused how wonderful it would be if corporations inspired such pride, so that employees viewed their workplaces not as hostile territory but as showplaces they wanted their friends to see. If workers felt that kind of ownership, lots of labor problems would evaporate. I don't think I am being naive. It happened on *Benfold*; why not in any other organization?

As we prepared to leave Melbourne, with the tugs alongside, I went down to the pier to make a final check on the mooring lines. I found a young woman crying uncontrollably.

"What's wrong?" I asked, though I had my suspicions.

"I can't believe how friendly your sailors are, and I just hate to see you leave. Especially Willie, who works in the radar room. Would you please give him a note from me?"

When I got back on board, I made an announcement over the PA system: "Now hear this, Willie in the radar room. I have a note to you from a lady whose heart you broke. Report to me on the bridge."

Willie duly appeared, blushing, and received his note as the whole crew cheered. From then on, he was considered a hero for having broken hearts beyond the call of duty in the Australian theater of operations. Maybe I should have awarded him a medal—not the Purple Heart, but the Valentine Cross, perhaps, with a chocolate cluster.

THE SECRET OF GOOD WORK? GOOD PLAY.

After we had mastered refueling at sea, we decided to try something harder—nighttime refueling at sea. Our first attempt worked flawlessly. It was easier than I expected, and a lot more pleasant than parboiling under a hot Gulf sun. My sailors liked it so much that from then on we always refueled at night.

Soon one sailor came up with the idea of enlivening night refueling by projecting music videos on the ship's rear bulkhead. That, in turn, inspired a laser light show. As we approached the fuel tanker, we would douse all our lights, blare the Olympic theme song (signifying we were the champions), and begin our laser show, followed by the music videos. All this entranced the tanker crews, who had the best seats in the house. After a while, those crews practically fought for the privilege of refueling *Benfold*.

Once the music videos were a hot ticket, we decided to add a live concert. Lieutenant K. C. Marshall was a talented singer and impersonator. We brought out the karaoke machine and set it up on deck. Six nights before Christmas 1997, we were ordered to refuel at midnight from the oiler *Seattle,* while the *Nimitz* refueled from its other side. As we steamed along drinking fuel, we entertained the other two ships with our flashing lights and blasting stereo. K. C. Marshall sang for about sixty minutes, doing inspired renditions of Elvis Presley. Marshall's version of "Blue Christmas" was really touching, as good as that song gets. Over on the *Nimitz* bridge, a veteran navigator, sad to be away for Christmas, wiped away tears.

That show cemented *Benfold*'s image throughout the fleet. We were the offbeat ship that wasn't afraid to loosen up, make the best of what had to be done, and share fun with everyone. Giving our people the freedom to act a little crazy seemed to confirm that we really cared about them. It boosted their pride in serving aboard a happening ship that others admired and envied. The entertainment paid huge dividends for everyone.

After leaving Australia, we were scheduled to refuel in Pago Pago, capital of American Samoa, on our way back to San Diego. We had all sorts of plans for that visit, highlighted by a beachside luau for which we had bought Australian beer and pigs to roast. The time is always right for a party. But no sooner had we pulled into Pago Pago than I was told to refuel, leave *Gary* and *Harry W. Hill* behind, and depart immediately for Seal Beach, California, to offload our Tomahawk missiles. Tomahawks were in such short supply in the Persian Gulf that ours were going to be flown straight back there as soon as we released them. That was the end of our luau. We handed all our beer and pigs over to *Harry W. Hill*'s crew, and they had our party. The ironic thing was that the senior leaders on *Hill* would never have dreamed up the idea of a luau in a million years.

Crossing the Pacific on the way to Seal Beach, my executive officer suggested we have a kite-flying contest. It wasn't the same as a pig roast, but we were used to making do on *Benfold*. The XO directed each division to create a kite from whatever materials could be found on the ship. The best flyer would win.

As we bypassed Hawaii, we ran into a dead calm. You could not float a kite, much less fly one. We zigzagged all over the ocean looking for a breath of wind. Eventually, I revved up all four engines to generate enough wind to get our kites aloft. Other Navy ships in the area spotted our peculiar maneuvers and shook their heads in bemusement—but we had our kite-flying contest, *Benfold* style.

All this shows what you can accomplish when you throw formality to the winds and free your people to have a life on your time, which soon becomes the time of their lives. None of this required big money, only imagination and goodwill.

On USS *Benfold,* the secret of good work was good play.

CHAPTER TWELVE

LIFE AFTER BENFOLD

🔱 My tour was over. It was time for me to hand over *Benfold* to its new captain.

A few weeks before the date, my commodore called and asked what time I wanted him to come aboard as guest speaker.

"Sorry," I said. "You aren't invited. This is just between me, my relief, my crew, and my ship. No one else is coming." In fact, instead of changing command in port and forcing the crew to do a lot of needless preparation, I had decided to turn over the ship at sea. The traditional change-of-command-in-port procedure is another dinosaur that needs extinction. Let me tell you about mine.

The commodore was pretty much used to me by now, and he came right back: "What do you want me to do with your medal?"

"Would you mind putting it in the mail, sir?"

On the Sunday night before we embarked, I had 310 live lobsters FedExed from Maine. For three days, we watched the lobsters in their tank on the mess decks. Most of my crew had never eaten a lobster or even seen one, so we gave lessons on how to get at the meat and eat it. Red Lobster gave us 310 bibs and claw-crackers, and on Wednesday night we had what I called my last supper: surf and turf.

Thursday morning we got up early and trained for four hours, because training was our job. Then at 10:45 we assembled on the flight deck in our coveralls—no fresh uniforms, just coveralls—and I gave the shortest change-of-command speech in military history. It was five words long: "You know how I feel." Then I saluted my relief and my crew. The new, improved *Benfold* was now theirs.

As I departed, I thought about how far we had all come in two years. Once divided and troubled, the ship I left to my successor was all a captain could wish for—the gem of the ocean. I was hugely proud of these sailors, who had become such a tight, accomplished, effective team, and I was unabashedly proud of myself. I had come far as both a leader and a person. I will never forget the excitement of commanding *Benfold,* of watching it improve every single day. I can't imagine a more rewarding job, and I would have done it for no pay. If I never match it again, I will still be the luckiest man alive, to have had such an experience.

People often ask why I didn't stay in the Navy. The answer is, I could have stayed. *Benfold* was such a success that I got the best evaluations of my life. The path was clear; I could have gone on to make admiral.

The problem was, the Navy's business is going to sea. In my first eighteen years in the Navy, I spent three full years sailing around the Persian Gulf. All told, I had acquired more sea time than any of my contemporaries from the Naval Academy. To stay on and go for admiral would have required three more six-month deployments, probably in a three-year time span.

Sea duty was rewarding. It also took a personal toll. In the end, I decided that as much as I loved the Navy, the people who worked for me, and my colleagues, it was time for me to move on. Now I want to share my experience and my journey to help others become better leaders.

The day before I was relieved, my successor took me aside and said he felt almost intimidated: *Benfold* was unlike anything in his experience. He did not want to be known as the one on whose watch *Benfold* had declined. He asked me what he should do. He had been raised by some real pit bulls since he joined the Navy, guys who truly believed in saluting those above and sweating those below. And here he was being thrown into a strange new situation where strict Navy tradition had been turned upside down. What should he do? Where should he begin?

I summarized the *Benfold* playbook, my recipe for running this phenomenal crew and ship. I tried not to sound like Moses, but my commandments were no less heartfelt. They were simply the chapter headings of this book: Lead by example; listen aggressively; communicate purpose and meaning; create a climate of trust; look for results, not salutes; take calculated risks; go beyond standard procedure; build up your people; generate unity; and improve your people's quality of life.

It took him a while to get all that, but in the end, he did.

A week after I left, he got his first real glimpse of what the ship was about. *Benfold* participated in a battle group exercise—a computer simulation, the first ever done entirely in port. Based in San Diego, the exercise revolved around the carrier *Constellation,* with two cruisers manning air defense and several destroyers, including *Benfold,* hunting enemy submarines.

It was the Navy's first attempt to show that quality training could be done with computers in port, at far less cost than it takes to send ships to sea. So this show was being eagerly watched at the highest levels in the Pentagon. If the exercise worked, simulated naval battles could save billions in the future. And to make the experiment credible, the exercise simulated even tougher conditions than the crews would encounter in most actual battles.

Benfold and the cruisers had essentially the same equipment, but the cruisers each had crews of about 440 compared with *Benfold*'s 310, mainly because they carried helicopters and needed additional specialists to run the carrier group's air defense. Given their special responsibility, the cruiser crews were considered senior to *Benfold*'s and were much more experienced in air defense operations. *Benfold* was supposed to defend only itself and to provide limited air defense to the rest of the battle group. And it had neither the ability nor the specialists to handle the entire group's air defense. But *Benfold* was "the little ship that could."

The two cruisers proved unready to fight the computer war and were forced to drop out of the exercise, one after the other. As disaster loomed, the battle group commander desperately ordered *Benfold* to take over as the air defense commander made a last-ditch effort to save the exercise. *Benfold* stepped up to the plate and performed flawlessly. It was a grand slam.

Benfold had demonstrated an ability it wasn't even supposed to have. It was an enormous victory for the crew, and truly iced their reputation. The admiral of the carrier battle group was astonished. I heard through third parties that he questioned his staff, unable to figure out how the cruisers could not even participate in the exercises while *Benfold,* the little guy, not only participated but led the whole game.

Six months after I left, *Benfold* got the highest grade in the history of the Pacific Fleet on the Combat Systems Readiness Review.

A year after I left, the ship was renominated for the Spokane Trophy, but came in second. That was a political decision. The admiral who made it had previously commanded the ship that won, and he gave them the prize. Of course I thought the *Benfold* was more deserving.

What kept *Benfold* going?

My successor became a great leader. He was so highly valued that he was ranked number one commanding officer in his squadron. *Benfold*'s retention rate was still triple the Navy's average, and other good things continued. In due course, the deputy commander in chief of the Atlantic Fleet chose him as executive assistant and pulled him off *Benfold* well ahead of his schedule. Moreover, he received the Legion of Merit award, which is typically reserved for senior captains and admirals.

I myself had gotten the lesser Meritorious Service Medal, and at first I was insanely jealous. But then I started to think, "Good for him." Here's a guy who demonstrated that he could change, that he could become a great leader. And good for the Navy to recognize his kind of achievement. Hopefully, he will hang around to earn his stars and cause positive change in the ranks of admirals. Furthermore, I was pleased that my crew helped facilitate his transformation.

The aftermath of my departure found *Benfold* sailing full steam ahead for at least the first year, and I am not shy about taking some of the credit. I believe that a leader's final evaluation should not be written until six months or a year after he or she leaves the organization. The true measure of how well you did on your watch is the legacy you hand your successors. And don't wish them ill so you can look good by contrast. Think bigger: Their success is actually your reward for leaving your command as shipshape as possible. As I write this, all of my officers and chief petty officers have transferred from ships and have gone on to other more demanding duties. Most of the crew has transferred as well.

We all feel satisfaction in a job well done, but the greatest satisfaction transcends personal achievement—it comes from helping others reach their potential. That's probably what keeps teachers going. It definitely kept me going during my tour on *Benfold*.

People ask how I got along with the other commanding officers. I have to be honest: less well than I should have. If one ship in a ten-ship group is doing conspicuously well, it's hard to imagine the other nine feeling good about it. Yet I never stopped to consider those feelings, which, of course, included my own competitiveness. That was a mistake on my part.

I certainly made life uncomfortable for the nine other commanding officers in my battle group. Their sailors would complain that *Benfold* was doing this or that, so why couldn't they? I was proud of our accomplishments, and to me it was logical for the other ships to simply adopt what we were doing. After all, top performance was what everyone was supposedly trying to achieve. That was one area where I failed to put myself in other people's shoes and see things their way. You might say I was arrogantly naive.

In hindsight, I could have been much more supportive of my colleagues—for example, by telling them in advance what we were doing, so they could join us voluntarily rather than having to be ordered to join us later.

Being compared unfavorably to *Benfold*—time after time— must have caused the wrong kind of competition. In my eyes, I was merely competing with myself to have the best ship possible. I never cared what the competition was doing. But in retrospect, it's obvious that they cared what we were doing, and they didn't like it one bit. I wish I had seen that at the time.

If you decide to go the *Benfold* route in your own organization, be warned: By doing new and innovative things, you may create jealousy and animosity. Try to be sensitive to that.

On the other hand, don't pull your punches just to avoid hurting your colleagues' feelings. Getting an entire group to excel is worth any number of offended peers. Maybe it is best simply to accept the fact that excellence upsets some people. It always has and always will. Live with it.

My approach to leadership on a Navy ship began as an experiment, born of necessity, but I have since found that it is far from unique. In all sorts of thriving businesses, the managerial role has changed from order-giver to people-developer, from authoritarian boss to talent cultivator. Nowadays, the most effective managers work hard at showing people how to find their own solutions, and then get out of their way. Given my responsibility for the very lives of my sailors, I could never go quite that far. But this book confirms how surprisingly far I was able to push Navy leadership in that direction. The reason was simple: It works.

I hope that my experience will enhance your own career, and that my improvised techniques will inspire you to invent even better ones. But let's not limit these hopes to our respective careers.

As this book goes to press, the United States and its allies have declared war on international terrorists, those secret predators both global and invisible, whose cruelties cannot be allowed to prevail. If anything is certain about this historic conflict, it is that it can't be won by the command-and-control culture that long sapped the creativity of too many American business and military organizations. In this war, ponderous armies and corporations, stalled by hubris and complacency, will be no more effective than Britain's vaunted Redcoats were in the American Revolution. Victory will go, as it did then, to the forces with the greatest horizontal leadership, the ones imbued with small-unit daring and initiative. That kind of self-starting leadership lies deep in the American grain, a legacy from the old rigors of frontier strife. Though seemingly leached out of the culture by large organizations, the upsurge of individuals risking their lives for others was the most awesome aspect of the World Trade Center catastrophe. To me, it reflected the vast reservoir of selflessness in the American character that leaders at every level must learn to tap for the common good. My own experience aboard *Benfold* suggests the potential of that spirit, once leaders learn how to release it. I therefore offer this book not only as your own career builder, but as a guide to showing people how to join in leading themselves for a purpose larger than themselves. That's the real *Benfold* story—the leadership lesson I hope you can soon apply to what-

ever organization you serve, civilian or military, beginning tomorrow.

Finally, let's all stipulate the winning leader's first principle:
Optimism rules. And the corollary: Opportunities never cease.

The bottom line: It's your ship. Make it the best.

EPILOGUE

BEYOND <u>BENFOLD</u>

⚓ IN OUR TIME, ORGANIZATIONS OFTEN BECOME TOO complex for their leaders to run effectively. Some beset leaders try to wriggle out of reality by ignoring chronic problems; others pit their subordinates against one another in so-called competition that winds up subverting any common purpose. The price of dysfunctional leadership is, of course, a dysfunctional organization.

During my Navy career, I found my own purpose in trying to create something better—leadership that truly earns its keep by taking full responsibility for solving killer problems.

Leadership is not a paycheck. Leadership is a calling. You have to want to lead with all the caring and energy of Ernest Shackleton conquering Antarctica or Moses parting the Red Sea. And you have to be accountable—no blame game is acceptable. The buck stops at the tip of your nose.

This book describes the leadership shortcomings that came about as a result of our resistance to change and improve in the Navy. During my own leadership transformation, I learned to fill it with methods that transformed my own complex organization, USS *Benfold*. Those methods lived on beyond my captaincy because they worked—and benefited every leader who used them.

After I left *Benfold* in 1999, for example, I took the liberty of e-mailing the three-star admiral who was responsible for the readiness of more than a hundred ships and facilities in the Pacific Fleet. I wanted to share what I had learned about reconnecting officers and sailors, and confronting other neglected areas as well. I urged the admiral to hold commanding officers personally responsible for the retention and disciplinary rates of their crews. Thank heaven for open-minded admirals: This one immediately focused his strong mind and will on ships with abnormally high turnovers. In no time, commanding officers got the message: Boost your retention rate or forget promotion.

It worked. Retention rates increased; unplanned discharges plummeted. It was also contagious. In 2001, reenlistments throughout the Navy rose by 20 percent. There was a sharp decrease in disciplinary problems and workers' compensation cases—and a dramatic boost in new enlistments. The lesson is inescapable. Once an issue becomes important to senior management, it becomes important down the chain of command. The results can be astonishing—newly loyal workers, better products, higher sales, and healthy profits. All because leaders do what they are paid to do—lead. In a nutshell, leaders are supposed to solve awful problems and inspire wonderful work. Ego-trippers need not apply.

In my post-*Benfold* life, I have been enormously pleased by the U.S. military's improved leadership. All four branches have increasingly rejected the inefficiency of interservice rivalry that duplicates weapons and squanders taxpayer dollars. Since the events of September 11, 2001, strong leadership has demanded interservice cooperation, thus multiplying force effectiveness with great results. Whatever your political views on the war in Afghanistan, the campaign itself has been a model of efficiency in what appeared to be highly unpromising terrain. The operational plan sought maximum results with minimal resources. By all reports thus far, the execution by U.S. airmen, sailors, soldiers, and marines has been flawless.

In business, I have encountered many companies with the kind of bad habits and poor leadership that troubled *Benfold* when I first went aboard. Too many company departments appear blind to what they could accomplish together. Bereft of good leadership, they are trapped in needless bickering, politics, and posturing, with predictable damage to the bottom line. And yet unity of purpose is quite achievable, even against heavy odds, and sometimes because of them. We created unity on *Benfold*. The U.S. military did it in Afghanistan. I am convinced that businesses everywhere can do the same. After all, it's our ship.

ACKNOWLEDGMENTS

I would like to thank my parents, Don and Mary, for the tremendous example of strength and commitment in their raising of the seven of us. Their wisdom, endurance, perseverance, and unconditional love gave each of us a solid foundation upon which much can be built.

I would like to thank Dr. William J. Perry for the opportunity of a lifetime. His support, patience, and guidance provided me many priceless lessons that made me both a better leader and shipmate. A special thanks to his "crack staff"—Earl Masters, Carol Chaffin, Cindy Baldwin, Marshall Williams, Bill Brown, and Rick Kisling—for countless laughs, support, and creating an extended family for me.

I am fortunate in so many ways, but this book would never have been written were it not for another former William Perry staff member—a Hoosier of great renown—Mr. Larry Smith, now with Business Executives for National Security (BENS). Larry heard about our leadership journey and introduced me to

ACKNOWLEDGMENTS

Ms. Polly LaBarre, the outstanding senior editor at *Fast Company* magazine who chronicled our Grassroots Leadership model. None of this would have ever been possible without Polly's wisdom and insight. Thanks, Polly.

I would like to acknowledge my Naval Academy roommates and lifelong friends, Roy Bishop and George Papaiouanou, who helped me make it when I didn't always want to. A special thanks to Michael Bolger for his unyielding guidance and unconditional support.

I would also like to thank my literary agent Helen Rees and the Wordworks, Inc., team—Donna Carpenter, Maurice Coyle, Susan Higgins, Deborah Horvitz, Larry Martz, Cindy Butler Sammons, and Robert Shnayerson. I also had the best editors ever. Rick Wolff, Dan Ambrosio, and Madeleine Schachter at Warner Books rounded the dream team who helped make this book a reality. Finally, I would like to thank my fiercely loyal assistant, David Lauer, for his valued and never-ending commitment on meeting the deadlines required for this book.

And a very special thanks to all of those in uniform who serve our great country.